Quick Study Commentary Series:
Romans

By Chad Sychtysz

© 2024 Spiritbuilding Publishers.
All rights reserved. No part of this book may be reproduced in any form without the written permission of the publisher.

Published by
Spiritbuilding Publishers
9700 Ferry Road, Waynesville, Ohio 45068

QUICK STUDY COMMENTARY SERIES
Romans
By Chad Sychtysz

ISBN: 978-1955285-87-2

Spiritbuilding
PUBLISHERS

spiritbuilding.com

Table of Contents

Introduction to *Romans* 1
Salutation and Introduction (1:1–17) 7

Section One: The Righteous Are Justified by Faith (1:18—4:25)
Gentiles Stand Guilty before God (1:18–32) 10
God Is an Impartial Judge (2:1–16) 16
Jews Also Stand Guilty before God (2:17–29) 20
All Have Sinned and Are Guilty before God (3:1–20) 22
We Are Justified by Grace through Faith (3:21–31) 24
Historical Examples of Justification by Faith (4:1–25) 27

Section Two: Benefits of Being Justified by Faith (5:1—8:39)
The Benefit of Peace with God (5:1–21) 30
The Benefit of Newness of Life (6:1–23) 36
The Benefit of Freedom from Law's Condemnation (7:1–25) 41
The Benefit of the Spirit's Guidance (8:1–17) 46
The Consolation of Hope and Divine Assurance (8:18–39) 51

A Recap of Romans 1—8 56

Section Three: The Righteousness of God (9:1—11:36)
God Has Not Failed in His Promises to Israel (9:1–33) 58
God's Righteousness Shown to Israel (10:1–21) 62
God's Righteousness Shown to Gentiles (11:1–36) 66

Section Four: The Righteousness of God Produces a Righteous Life (12:1—15:33)
Righteous Conduct toward Fellow Christians (12:1–21) 71
Righteous Conduct toward Secular Government (13:1–14) 76
Righteous Conduct of the Strong and Weak (14:1—15:13) 80
A Proper Regard for Paul's Ministry (15:14–33) 84
Paul's Greetings and Final Admonitions (16:1–27) 87
Appendix: Calvinism (aka Doctrine of Predestination) 91
Sources Used for *Romans Quick Study Commentary* 100
Endnotes 102

Introduction to *Romans*

There is no single book in the New Testament (NT) which provides as much detail and insight into Christian theology as *Romans*. This epistle delves into several critical themes: salvation, grace, mercy, faith, justification by faith, sin, redemption, man's free will, God's sovereign decisions, indwelling of the Holy Spirit, etc. It also provides practical application of these doctrines in the sphere of everyday Christian life (chapters 12—15). *Romans* is perhaps "the most significant theological letter ever written"[1] and "is widely regarded as the most significant of Paul's letters."[2] Martin Luther called it "the chief part of the New Testament and the very purest Gospel."[3] Indeed, without it, our understanding of divine grace and the appropriate human response to that grace would be fragmented and incomplete.

However, as with all doctrinal treatises, *Romans* is admittedly an involved study.[4] The fact that Paul took eight chapters to explain one statement, "the righteous man shall live by faith" (1:17), indicates that this is not going to be a casual read. Parts of *Romans* (e.g., 2:12–15; 5:12–18; or 7:14–25) are among the most difficult to understand in the entire NT. The underlying complexities and implications of such passages can be intimidating even to the seasoned Bible student (see 2 Peter 3:15–16). Commentators, lexicographers, and scholars have wrestled with these same passages, and such men are not always in agreement. It is likely that we, too, will wrestle with these; we also may not reach a consensus.

This does not mean that Christians should avoid the study of *Romans*. In it, Paul outlines the very basis for our relationship with God. He explains how (and why) an all-powerful God can and will accept into His fellowship those who are deserving of death. He also explains, in a manner unique to the NT, how the sinner is made righteous in God's sight. *Romans* also addresses the status of Israel: why Israel was chosen to be God's people; why the Law of Moses could not justify Israel; and what has happened to this relationship considering the gospel of Christ. These are not only important questions to the Jews of Paul's day; they bear directly upon God's faithfulness to all who are in covenant with Him.

Romans was written ca. AD 57. (Some scholars set the date as early as 56, others as late as 59.) The apostle Paul is unanimously accepted as its author. "The canonicity [i.e., recognition as a legitimate and inspired part of the NT] of Romans was never an issue in the Church. From the earliest beginnings of the formation of the NT canon its place within it has been secure …"[5]

It is likely that Paul wrote this treatise during his three-month stay in Corinth (in Achaia) during his third missionary journey (Acts 18:23ff), while waiting to return to Jerusalem after a lengthy absence.[6] Having collected money for about a year from among the (predominantly) Gentile churches throughout Macedonia and Achaia, Paul's mission was to provide that money as benevolence toward the famine-stricken Christians in Jerusalem. After this important delivery, which also served to symbolize solidarity between Jewish and Gentile Christians, he had every intention of visiting the Christians in Rome (15:22–29). Unfortunately for him, Paul's plans were shattered when he was arrested in Jerusalem on a false premise and, after spending some two years in jail in Caesarea, Paul was sent to Rome as a prisoner, not as a free man (Acts 21—28).[7]

The many salutations in chapter 16 indicate that Paul was already acquainted with several brethren in Rome. The church there probably consisted of several small house-congregations, as was likely the case in Corinth or Jerusalem; Paul collectively addressed these brethren as one group ("to all who are beloved of God in Rome, called as saints"—1:7). The church there was predominantly Gentiles, although Paul gives special attention to the Jews since the Jewish system was about to end. Paul's preaching of the gospel consistently emphasized "no distinction" in God's sight between ethnicities or nationalities (Gal. 3:27–29, Eph. 2:13–18), but this does not mean there was no occasion in Scripture in which specific groups (or their concerns) could be addressed.

Theme and Purpose: The theme of *Romans* is undoubtedly "the righteous man shall live by faith" (1:17). God first used this expression to the prophet Habakkuk to declare what He sought from Israel (Hab. 2:4). Paul not only expounded upon this expression but explained that it is the foundational premise upon which every soul—both Jew and Gentile—is saved. The first eight chapters of *Romans* deal directly with this question in a manner that highlights Paul's intense rabbinical training. The next several chapters (9—11) address the Jews considering this statement: If the Jews were given the Law of Moses, then how are they saved by faith? The Gentiles also had questions that needed to be answered: Did God keep His promises with Israel—and will He keep His promises with us? Does the inclusion of Gentiles into the salvation of God put them on par with the Jews, or is Christianity just another form of Judaism? Was God responsible for making the Jews unfaithful, or was God faithful in dealing with "hardened" Jews?

Both Jews and Gentiles needed to know exactly where they stood with God and with each other in this new world order called Christianity. Undoubtedly Paul had been dealing with these questions wherever he went; by inspiration of the Holy Spirit, he chose to explain them fully in his correspondence with the Christians at Rome. (There is a practical reason for this: since Rome was the intersection of the world at that time, his writing would be quickly and easily dispersed abroad by sending it there.)

In the final chapters (12—15), Paul provides a practical explanation of how those who live by faith ought to conduct themselves, especially toward their fellow brethren, world governments, the "weak," and all men. Paul ends with a lengthy salutation, as well as necessary warnings and final admonitions to Christians in Rome.

More specifically, some themes in *Romans* (often running concurrently) include the following:

- Without question, **faith** is the dominant theme of *Romans*. Faith's power always lies outside of the one possessing it: faith by itself can do nothing, but faith in an all-powerful God has no limits. Being "justified by faith" refers to God's acceptance of the condemned sinner's plea for mercy, which appeals to the redemptive work of Jesus Christ. Paul never reduces faith to a mere concept, however, but consistently (in all his epistles) defines it as an active demonstration of one's obedience to God. No one can come to God without faith; God defines faith as an appropriate response to whatever He wills to be done (Mat. 7:21).
- Paul spends a great deal of time talking about **grace**, even though he only infrequently uses the actual word. Saving grace is, in essence, everything that God does to compensate for human inadequacies and weaknesses regarding salvation. Put another way: grace is whatever God does that we cannot do to be saved. Christians need to know how a holy God can have fellowship with sinful people. This process needs to be explained considering law and grace: we need to know the relationship between these two things, and how they both affect human salvation. If we are justified by faith, then what need is there for law? But if we are required to keep God's laws, then what is the role of saving grace? These are significant and timeless doctrinal questions; ultimately, every single Christian needs to come to terms with them.[8]
- **"Law"** is one of the more profound concepts of the entire epistle of *Romans*. Law provides a legal standard of expected behavior from

believers and unbelievers alike. Sin cannot be "imputed" or charged in the absence of divine law (4:15). Those who are not "in Christ" are under what might be called a universal moral law, which conforms to God's divine nature (see comments on. 2:12–16). Those who *are* "in Christ" (i.e., Christians) are under "the law of the Spirit of life" (8:2), a.k.a. "the law of Christ" (Gal. 6:2). Freedom in Christ does not mean freedom from obedience because obedience is necessary to demonstrate faith. Christians are "not under law but under grace" (6:14), but this speaks to how they are *justified* by God—by *grace*, not perfect *law-keeping*—not to exempt them from obedience to law.

- **Works** (in the context of the NT) refers to any act of human will. These acts may be in response to God's word or merely attempts at self-justification. Works can be visible (Mat. 5:16) or invisible (John 6:29), natural (human actions) or supernatural (divine actions), moral (righteous) or immoral (unrighteous). Works can also refer to any system of justification by which a person is either approved or condemned, according to whatever that system demands or imposes. Works are required by the believer to prove his faith in God (James 2:26), even though the works themselves do not save him (Eph. 2:8–9).[9]

- **Fellowship** is implied in any discussion of grace since this is its ultimate objective. God desires fellowship with every person, but this is impossible without a soul's faithful surrender to His will. The union of human faith and divine grace creates "newness of life" (6:4). Our good works (in obedience to God's commandments) are not enough: good behavior is a characteristic of one who is in fellowship with God, not a definition of or replacement for fellowship. In *Romans*, Paul lays the groundwork for our fellowship with God and defines what is required from both God and the believer for this to exist.

- God's **sovereignty** [lit., "sole rule"] is another sub-theme of *Romans*. This is covered both directly (chapters 9—11) and indirectly. Because of whom He is, God has the prerogative to make decisions based upon His omniscience and absolute authority. Some have assumed that God's divine sovereignty thus overrules human free will. This is the basis for modern Calvinism (see Appendix 1), which teaches that God preselects (or predestines the eternal disposition of) every person prior to birth. While Paul does teach that Christ's church is predestined for glory (8:29), he nowhere teaches that God takes full responsibility for a person's salvation or his spiritual ruin. If God *did* take such

- **Hope** is mentioned in *Romans* more often than in any other (NT) book. Paul repeatedly refers to hope as a matter of Christian doctrine and inspiration. For the believer, hope takes the place of the emptiness of Roman or Greek idolatry and paganism (Gal. 4:8–9, Eph. 2:11–12, and 1 Thess. 1:9). One is condemned and without hope who has broken the moral laws of God; yet "there is therefore now no condemnation for those who are in Christ Jesus" (8:1). This hope is real and life-changing; it encourages the believer and demands action (for a positive result).
- **Sin** is the deliberate, active transgression of God's will (divine law), whether the action is physical (visible) or psychical (mental). By necessity, the presence of sin demands the presence of a law which has been violated (3:20, 4:15, and 5:13). One who commits sin becomes a sinner; this action directly and immediately affects the status of the one who performed it. All people have become sinners (3:23) who are mentally competent to know the difference between right and wrong and are morally accountable to God for their actions. Sin condemns, corrupts, and destroys; nothing good ever comes from it. Apart from divine redemption, every sinner will be destroyed for having corrupted the sacred soul which God had entrusted to him.
- Paul also uses the word "**flesh**" many times in all his writings. "Flesh" can have different meanings, depending upon the context in which it is used. First, it can refer to what we are made of ("flesh and blood"—Eph. 2:11, Col. 1:22). Second, it can refer to one's body or his identity as a human being (1 Cor. 6:16, Gal. 4:13). Third, it can refer to our earthly human nature that stands in opposition to God's own divine nature; in this sense it is collectively referred to as the unconverted "world" (1 John 2:15–17).[10] A person who is only "of the flesh" is hostile toward God, is not saved, and cannot save himself (8:6–9). Paul often refers to a person's physical (earthly) body as the manifestation of human disobedience (since it is under a curse—Gen. 3:17–19). In other words, since a person's body is corrupted by moral disobedience, and that which is corrupted must be destroyed or redeemed (1 Cor. 15:50), Paul speaks in *Romans* of the "body of death" (7:24) or the "sinful flesh" (8:3).
- **Justification** is undoubtedly one of Paul's major themes in *Romans*. To be justified by something (or someone) means to be in right agreement (i.e., just) to whatever standard is used to make that determination.

In the case of one's salvation, it is the legal process by which a human soul is pronounced innocent according to God's divine standard of righteousness (see below). A sinless person needs no justification; a sinner can only be justified by the blood (life) of a perfect sacrifice that is offered in his place. The basis for a sinner's justification, then, lies outside of his own ability—through the redemptive work of Jesus Christ (3:23–25). Yet, no one will be justified by God who does not put his faith in Christ's ability to save him.

- **Righteousness**, in Christian theology, works concurrently with justification. If one is justified, then he is righteous; if he is righteous, then he must (already) be justified. Both terms involve a right relationship with God, a person having satisfied what God requires for that fellowship to exist. Righteousness is a condition, status, or judgment (decision) conferred upon the believer by God.[11] In a sense, it is a legal pronouncement of divine approval (4:3); it is God's verdict of a person's state of being based his faith and demonstrated by his obedience. There are only two ways in which righteousness can be achieved: one's own worthiness, or the worthiness of another who is Himself proven worthy.[12]

- **Sanctification** (or holiness) refers to the process by which a person is consecrated by or made holy to God. Paul teaches in *Romans* that one can only be sanctified when two factors are simultaneously present: God's grace and a believer's faith. Justification is what God does *for* the believer, in the absence of his ability; sanctification is what God does *to* him (or in him) for fellowship to exist between the two parties. The Holy Spirit is directly involved in the sanctification process (8:6–9). The purpose behind sanctification is to set a person apart (*to* God and *from* the world) to offer a priest-like ministry—thus, the "living and holy sacrifice" terminology in 12:1–2.

- Finally, a dominant theme (in the latter part of *Romans*) is each Christian's **acceptance of one another**. Chapter 14 deals almost entirely with how one strong in faith should properly regard one weak in faith. ("Strong" here means learned or mature, not arrogant or unchallengeable; "weak" means unlearned or spiritually immature, not unwilling or lazy.) Our mutual respect "in Christ" is one of the hallmarks of those who are justified by faith. We would be at a tremendous loss without Paul's valuable exposition on this subject.

Salutation and Introduction (1:1–17)

Paul begins his epistle to the Romans with a powerful description of his own office as well as that of Christ (1:1–2).[13] He immediately defends and provides authority for his apostleship, claiming to be "set apart for the gospel of God" (see Gal. 1:11–16).[14] An "apostle" is literally "one sent forth or away with orders."[15] The term can be used generally (as in Acts 14:14 regarding Barnabas) or specifically (as Paul uses the term here). Christ's apostles were all ordained ("called") by Christ Himself, having been entrusted with His gospel to preach and defend as His personal ambassadors (cf. Acts 26:16–18).

Though he is an apostle, Paul regards himself also as a "bond-servant" [Greek, *doulos*] of Christ. Since Rome was filled with slaves, many of whom were educated even more than their own masters, Paul reminds the Romans that he also is a slave to the Highest Master. Thus, he immediately identifies with the slave population of the Roman Empire by stating, in essence, "I, too, am a slave—to Christ, not to mere men." Later, he will state that all Christians must voluntarily become "slaves to righteousness" to serve the Living God (6:16–18).

Paul then defines the two-fold nature of Christ (1:3–4): according to the flesh, He is "a descendant of David"; according to heaven, He is "the Son of God."[16] If Jesus was not truly the anticipated Christ/Messiah of Old Testament (OT) prophecy, He could not be Israel's King. He also could not have fulfilled (and thus, given closure to) the covenant between God and Israel. Similarly, if He is not the Son of God, He is an impostor and speaks without authority. If His divinity remained unproven, then all the promises He made to believers are not to be believed. Thus, it is imperative that Paul begins with these two facts: Jesus is the Christ *and* the divine Son of God (Mat. 16:16, John 20:31). This has been substantiated through divine prophecy, John the Baptist's testimony, Jesus' supernatural signs and miracles (most notably His resurrection from the dead), and God's own testimony (Mat. 3:17, 17:5, and John 12:28).

Since he will be outlining some of the most important theological ideas that have ever been revealed from heaven, it is critical that Paul's authority be legitimized. He says, in essence: "I have been directly commissioned by Jesus Christ, who is a legitimate heir to the throne of David and at the same time the Son of the Living God Himself, to reveal to you this message." Having established his apostolic authority, Paul's first proclamation is both powerful and positive: he identifies the Roman Christians as "the called of Christ" (1:6), "beloved of God," and "saints" (1:7).[17] Their relationship with God was unquestioned; the rest of the epistle will deal with *how* that relationship came to be and what is expected of them since they are in it.[18]

Paul's Personal Remarks (1:8–15): Before proceeding to doctrinal matters, Paul first takes a moment to address these Christians on a personal level (1:8–15). He was anxious to see them; it was his full intention to make a brief visit to Rome on his way to Spain (see 15:22–29).[19] It was also his intention to "impart some spiritual gift" to them (1:11)—i.e., to lay his hands upon them for the purpose of giving them miraculous gifts. Such is the necessary implication, based on similar situations (Acts 8:14–17, 19:1–6, 2 Tim. 1:6, etc.). This also implies that no apostle had yet been to Rome to perform this; otherwise, it would be pointless for Paul to mention it.[20] Whatever gift Paul had in mind, it was for the purpose of establishing (or strengthening) the Christians in Rome. He apologized, in a way, for not having already seen them, yet clarified that it was not for lack of desire but of time and opportunity (1:13). He was "eager" to preach to them in Rome but already had a full schedule as an apostle of Christ and ambassador to the Gentiles (Eph. 3:8-10).

Paul's Thesis: Justification by Faith (1:16-17): In 1:16-17, Paul begins an important theological discussion that will cover the next ten chapters. Despite the low opinion some people had of him (see 1 Cor. 4:8-13, 2 Cor. 10:10, etc.), Paul was "not ashamed of the gospel" (1:16).[21] "Ashamed" is probably two-fold: first, Paul had no reason to be embarrassed by who he was (a Christian) or what he preached (the gospel). Second, he would not be disappointed or experience regret for having accepted this responsibility (cf. Mark 10:29-30). The Greek word for "ashamed" can mean either or both thoughts, and is used both ways in the NT.

The gospel is not a mere message of intellectual stimulation or entertaining myths (cf. Acts 17:16-21) but of "salvation"—a state of existence that is entirely beyond human ability to achieve by one's own strength or wisdom. Paul emphasizes the supernatural "power" of this message: the power to regenerate a dead soul (Eph. 2:1). "Power of God"[22] is not applied to the mere *words* of the gospel, as though the Bible has regenerating power of its own. Rather, it is in the "living and enduring word of God" (1 Peter 1:23)—i.e., the divine message of the Holy Spirit, which, when obeyed, calls for divine grace to heal an otherwise helpless human soul. This "word of God"—the "message of truth" and "gospel of your salvation" (Eph. 1:13)—is the work of God the Father, God the Son, and God the Spirit. This power is universal in scope: it is available to Jews and non-Jews alike. Yet, it remains particular or conditional in its application: it is given only to those who "believe." To "believe" necessarily requires a surrender of one's will and the demonstration of obedient faith. While no one is saved *by* his works, to believe in God *is* a required work of faith (John 6:29).

The expression "to the Jew first" indicates that the gospel has been revealed methodically, in a certain sequential order. The "kingdom of God" which Jesus preached was directed only to the Jews for good reason: entrance into God's kingdom was the culmination of promises made to the kingdom of Israel. The fact that many Jews did not accept Jesus as their King—and thus rejected this invitation—did not diminish the power of the kingdom or God's decision to invite "the Jew first" (see Acts 13:45-47). "Greek" here can mean a Greek-speaking person, a cultured (Hellenistic) Greek, or simply a non-Jew (i.e., a Gentile); perhaps all these meanings can apply here, as the context seems very general. In short, this gospel is available to the entire world, to "whoever believes in Him" (John 3:16).

"For in it [i.e., the gospel] the righteousness of God is revealed" (1:17)—that is, God's fairness, justice, grace, and mercy are all made supremely evident within this message of salvation. "Before salvation can be completed, righteousness must be manifested. God, the righteous judge, must do righteous judgment in his court; and, in this court, man must secure the verdict, Righteous."[23] God's faithfulness—to His word, His promises, and us—is possible only because He is righteous (and vice versa). Whenever Paul says, "God is faithful" (1 Cor. 1:9), he is also saying, "God is righteous," for it is impossible for Him to be one without the other.

Righteousness cannot be reckoned (credited) apart from human faith, nor can it be reckoned before this faith is expressed in the form of obedience. While righteousness is not a compensation (or payment) for faith, it is impossible for God to save a person who is capable of faith yet refuses to exercise it. In 1:17, Paul speaks of two parties that are "righteous": God and those justified by their faith in Him. The fact that Paul quotes from Hab. 2:4 indicates that this is not a new teaching—it is not exclusive to the gospel of Christ—but has *always* been how sinners have been justified to God: through *faith*, not mere works, good intentions, or any other means.

SECTION ONE:

THE RIGHTEOUS ARE JUSTIFIED BY FAITH (1:18—4:25)

Gentiles Stand Guilty before God (1:18–32)

To establish that only God can justify a "righteous man," Paul must prove that a person cannot be justified in any other way. If a person is capable of self-justification, then he would not need God. Yet, human history has proved that attempts at justification by any other means—by human effort, human wisdom, human laws, or idolatry—have failed miserably. For a person to be justified by God, however, he must have knowledge of the standard of justification (i.e., God's revealed will). He must also come to terms with his own spiritual inadequacy: in his unjustified state of being, he stands condemned before God.

Paul begins this discussion by stating two fundamental truths revealed from heaven: God's righteousness, which leads to a person's salvation; and His wrath against unrighteousness, which leads to a person's condemnation (1:18–20). Before discussing salvation, Paul first expounds upon one's awful predicament for having abandoned God's righteousness. While his comments concern "men" in general, Paul refers to heathens and pagans specifically—i.e., Gentiles who, in past ages, have been "excluded from the commonwealth of Israel," and who had "no hope" and were "without God in the world" (Eph. 2:12).[24] These men "knew God" (1:21) and His "ordinances" (i.e., God's unwritten but necessarily-implied moral laws; see 1:32), but they still did not obey Him. These ordinances (or moral laws) pre-date even the Law of Moses, extending back to "the creation of the world" (see notes on 5:13).

The Consequences of Unbelief (1:18–32): Someone may ask, "Just how much did the ancient people know about God anyway?"[25] The scope of this information was small in comparison to what we know today. Nonetheless, God had provided sufficient evidence in the physical creation and in man's moral nature to warrant putting one's faith in Him. Concerning a person's self-inspection, it would be clear that:

- Human beings are the highest form of life on earth.
- Human intelligence is superior to any other intelligence on earth.
- Human enterprise and creativity are superior to any other animate activity on earth.
- Humans can reason, discern, communicate, emote, and create far beyond the level of any other earthly animalistic life.
- While animals operate by instinct and (to a limited degree) learned behavior, humans operate according to a sense of justice and morality that they can temporarily circumvent but cannot remove.
- Humans have a consciousness of themselves that transcends their physical bodies; this spiritual awareness permeates every race, culture, and historical epoch ever known.
- This spiritual awareness also compels human beings to give worship to a higher being (real or imagined), as a means of validating and giving meaning to their existence.

Such qualities are evident in all people; they are meant to lead us to seek out our Creator. We should not assume that physical or moral evidence alone can prove the sovereignty and omnipotence of God. Paul does not say, "That which *may* be known" about God but "that which *is* known" about Him.[26] God has always provided a reason to believe in Him—and thus to put one's faith in Him (Heb. 11:6). As Paul said in Athens (Acts 17:25–28):

> He [God] Himself gives to all people life and breath and all things; and He made from one man every nation of mankind to live on all the face of the earth, having determined their appointed times and the boundaries of their habitation, that they would seek God, if perhaps they might grope for Him and find Him, though He is not far from each one of us; for in Him we live and move and exist. ...

God has revealed Himself through physical nature (i.e., things that have "been made"; see Heb. 3:4), transcendent morality, and human consciousness. He has also revealed Himself through His own Presence (Gen. 18:1ff, John 12:28–30, etc.), heavenly angels (Heb. 13:2), prophets (Heb. 1:1), law (Deut. 29:29), and His own Son (Acts 17:30–31, Heb. 1:2). Regardless of how (or how much) people knew of God, Paul's point is still valid: those who deny the observable and known evidence concerning God's existence are "without excuse" (1:20).

This means that such people have no legitimate claim to insurmountable ignorance, nor can they justify their disobedience. To "suppress" truth does not mean merely to ignore or fail to act upon it, but to hold it down—i.e., to "prevent truth from exerting its power in the heart and the life."[27] We might picture a person holding someone's head underwater to drown him: such is what people have tried to do, in effect, with the truth about God. Thus, it is a deliberate and malicious action, not an unconscious response. Yet, truth will not die, and it cannot be killed.

In suppressing the truth about God, people abandon all hope of spiritual enlightenment or self-improvement. Their unconverted minds descend into animalistic desires and pleasures. What begins as moral apostasy inevitably leads to deviant and self-destructive behavior (1:21–23):

- they knew God, but
- they did not honor Him, which meant
- they did not give Him thanks (i.e., were ungrateful), and thus
- they became futile (useless or vain) in their speculations—i.e., their own self-determined, mythological explanations of how they and the world came to be, etc., were unfounded, self-serving, and often absurd; thus
- their foolish heart—which was *made* foolish by having rejected the Source of its reason and intellect—was darkened, so that
- they worshiped nature (the creation of God) rather than God Himself, and images (idols) of gods of their own making.

Paganism and heathenism are not original religions of men but are themselves apostasies from the true religion of God.[28] "Darkness" (i.e., ignorance, depravity, and wickedness) indicates the absence of God's divine influence, spiritual enlightenment, and objective reality (cf. Luke 11:33–36, John 3:18–21, and Eph. 4:17–19). People who persistently refuse the light of God become immersed in a thick moral darkness in which they can no longer function as rational, spiritual human beings but are reduced to hedonistic, inhumane, and barbaric creatures. God's morality[29] becomes so diluted with self-indulgence that it loses all positive influence. Such people become fixated with self-gratification at any expense, regardless of the consequences. Thus, a darkened heart leads invariably to a darkened life—and a dreaded, hopeless future.

"Professing to be wise, they became fools" (1:22)—an ironic and profound indictment.[30] People who turn away from God always think they are *wise* for doing so; in some cases, the idea of a divine Creator is beneath them and is cause for ridicule and scoffing. (This attitude is common in modern atheism.) Such "wisdom" is "earthly, natural, and demonic"; it creates "disorder and every evil thing" (James 3:15–16); it is morally and logically inferior to a healthy belief in God. Worshiping the *creation* rather than the *Creator* is a massive self-deception (1:23).[31] "For if anyone thinks he is something when he is nothing, he deceives himself" (Gal. 6:3).

Three times in this passage (1:24–32) we read that "God gave them over" to something far worse than that which the unconverted pagans began. As people abandon the truth of God, they also abandon the providential restraints that keep them from behaving like animals rather than those made in God's image. This cannot mean that God tempted them to do evil (James 1:13) but that He allowed them to believe their lies as though they were true (2 Thess. 2:10–12). "[These] words sound to us like clods [of dirt] on the coffin as God leaves men to work their own wicked will."[32]

This moral abandonment always leads to sexual immorality and sexual deviancy, which are sins against one's own body as well as God Himself (1 Cor. 6:16–18). "When a people cease to respect God, they will not long respect their own bodies. They give themselves up to passions of dishonor."[33] This passage is nothing short of an explicit condemnation of effeminacy (of men) and homosexuality among both men and women. While many people today have desperately tried to downplay, reinterpret, or simply ignore this passage, it remains God's strong denouncement of these practices. Thus, we see a typical digression:

- ❏ people sin against God by means of idolatry (of any kind), leading to
- ❏ sins against one's own body, which leads to and often involves (in mutual fornication)
- ❏ sins against one's fellow man.

"Natural functions" in this context refers to sexual identity and relationships that God established in the Creation (i.e., the natural order of things). God did not create women to have sexual relations with women, nor men…with men. "Unnatural" means that which God never intended; defiance against the natural order; corruptions of the image of God. In the Law of Moses, the mating of two incompatible things was an abomination against God simply because it defied (and corrupted) the natural order (Lev. 18:22–23, Deut. 22:5, 9–11). It is immoral for a man to "burn" with passion toward or have sex with another man because this desecrates the natural order and defies the One who created it.[34] Such perverse mating creates an unholy union; such unions incur God's wrath and punishment.[35] The only sexual union that God established in the beginning is between a man and a woman within the context of marriage (Gen. 2:24; see 1 Cor. 7:2). This union is holy (sanctioned by God); the marriage of a man and a woman forms the basic building block of society; and this union agrees with the ultimate spiritual union of Christ and His church (Eph. 5:31–32).

Having defiled themselves, those who abandon God then defile all those around them (1:28–32). "Depraved" (1:28) means unfit, rejected (by God), or reprobate: in having rejected God, men are rejected by God.[36] In this divine rejection, such men are "given" or "handed over" to pursue their rotten vice.[37] They are "filled with" (1:29) all sorts of godless and self-serving behaviors, all of which seek personal advancement or pleasure at the expense of someone else—and their own souls. Most of the crimes mentioned here (1:29–31) are self-evident; many of them are closely related; similar lists of vices are found in Gal. 5:19–21 and 2 Tim. 3:1–7.

- "unrighteousness"—the Greek word here [*adikia*] implies something unjust or unequal, namely, something that violates God's justice or inequality.[38] Paul describes (in the first four vices mentioned here) a filled-to-the-brim depravity, a full measure (Prov. 1:31).
- "wickedness" here indicates something harmful, malicious, and grievous.[39]
- "greed": a desire for evil gain; a form of covetousness, "which amounts to idolatry" (Col. 3:5).
- "evil" (or maliciousness; licentiousness): in essence, anything opposed to or in defiance of God's goodness.
- "envy": an evil desire for what someone else has as a possession, talent, position, etc.
- "murder": from a root Greek word meaning "to slay," as in a selfish taking of another's life.[40]
- "strife": contention, wrangling (over something), or unnecessary friction between two or more people as the result of selfish ambitions (1 Cor. 3:3, 2 Cor. 12:20, Titus 3:9, etc.).
- "deceit": lit., something used as bait or trickery to purposely mislead someone.[41]
- "malice": lit., a bad character; malignity; mischievousness.[42]
- "gossips": lit., a whisperer; to speak secretly into the ear.[43] Namely,

"Those who secretly, and in a sly manner, by hints and innuendoes, detract from others, or excite suspicion of them."[44] The Greek word here [*psithuristes*] is not Paul's usual word for "gossips" [which is *diabolos*, "devil-talk"]; however, all gossip is satanic in nature.
- "slanderers": lit., backbiters, defamers, one who talks back (in contempt).[45]
- "haters of [or hateful toward] God": used in the passive sense here, that is, not actively seeking to hate God, but obviously hating Him by way of pursuing those things that oppose Him.[46]
- "insolent": lit., to give insult to; in 1 Tim. 1:13, Paul uses the same word, which is translated in the NASB as "violent aggressor."
- "arrogant": putting or vaunting oneself above others—common of human pride.
- "boastful": from a Greek word [*alazon*] referring to a vagabond, a wanderer, and (thus) like a traveling salesman of old that falsely brags about his wares, potions, cures, etc.; used only here and in 2 Tim. 3:2.
- "inventors of evil [things]": those who look for new or creative ways to be wicked; used only here in the NT.
- "disobedient to parents": in defiance of God's moral law concerning one's father and mother (Exod. 20:12; see Deut. 21:18–21). Disobedience to God naturally leads to disobedience to (or disrespect for) earthly authorities as well. Clearly, this is not talking about young(er) children, but those who remain at home and are old enough to be morally accountable to God. It can also be a charge against those who disregard their aging parents, the "disobedience" really being toward what God has commanded rather than toward the parents' instructions (as in Mark 7:9–13).
- "lacking in understanding": from the same Greek word rendered "foolish" in 1:21.
- "untrustworthy": lit., a covenant-breaker; unfaithful to a promise made; one who cannot be trusted to honor that to which he commits.
- "unloving": from a Greek word [*astorge*] which literally means "not having natural [or, familial] affection."[47] The Greeks had five words for "love": *agape, phileo, philadelphia, eros,* and *storge* (love of kindred). Four of these words are in the NT (*eros* is not); *storge* only appears here, and only in the negative sense (i.e., the absence of kindred love).
- "unmerciful": being destitute of compassion toward one's fellow human being. "As a proof of this we may remark, that no provisions for the poor

or infirm were made among the heathen. The sick and the infirm were cast out, and doomed to depend on the stinted charity of individuals."[48]

Such a list paints a truly awful picture of human depravity. When God's revelation has been rejected, there is no refinement or inducement to do what is good (Eph. 4:17–19, 2 Thess. 2:10–12). "A revelation from God … does not plant in the human heart a consciousness of right and wrong, but it does guide and refine that consciousness, and places motives before man to induce him to do right."[49] Chronic resistance, suppression, and sheer defiance of the truth never leads one to enlightenment; instead, such people descend further and deeper into moral darkness.[50] Even though such men "know the ordinance [law] of God," they do not care about God or His laws (1:32). In fact, they applaud and give full support to those who are like them (1 John 4:5).

God Is an Impartial Judge (2:1–16)

In chapter one, Paul began demonstrating the need for people to be justified by faith in God. The ancients were not justified by their own good behavior; some other means of justification was necessary. Having abandoned the guidance of divine law, men descended into satanic wickedness of every kind. God "gave them over" to their lawless desires to the point that they became animalistic in nature. (The truth is that they descended even *below* animalism: even animals obey their God-given instincts; and not even animals practice homosexuality.)

Now Paul turns to the Jewish people. The "you" here (in 2:1) is meant most generally, as referring to any person. The ancient Gentiles were a spiritually ignorant, morally deficient, and idolatrous people, to be sure. But the Jews, taken as a whole, were hardly better. Jesus called them "an evil and adulterous generation" (Mat. 12:39), a "brood of vipers" (Mat. 12:34), worshipers of money (Luke 16:14), and condescending toward sinners (Luke 18:9). The Jews were quick to "judge"—here, meaning condemn—the Gentiles' sins, yet they had many of their own sins. God would not judge only the Gentiles' sins, but the Jews' sins as well (2:2–3).

In any case, the expected response to God's revealed law—however that law is expressed—is repentance and obedience (2:4). One's stubborn resistance to God's kindness, mercy, and patience is inexcusable. God's kindness is not extended without purpose; it is designed to elicit a proper response from the one to whom it is shown (2 Peter 3:9). Since the Israelites had a much greater opportunity to learn of God's kindness (through His covenant with them), they ought to have responded differently than did pagans and heathens. As it was, many Jews (and possibly even Gentile moralists) condemned the pagans and heathens even while being guilty of their own crimes—in some cases, even the same crimes as those whom they condemned. Those who have a better knowledge of what is expected of them, yet practice sinful behavior anyway, are held even more responsible than others (see Luke 12:47–48 and James 3:1). One who knows the law cannot plead ignorance of it; therefore, he has "no excuse" for his crimes, just as the ancient Gentiles were "without excuse" (recall 1:20).

God Is an Impartial Judge (2:5–11): Regarding salvation or condemnation, God is fair and impartial to all people, regardless of their nationality or ethnicity (2:5–11).[51] He judges every person according to a just and equitable standard, one which is known to those who are being judged by it. The outcome of such judgment will be dependent upon each person's response to "the truth" (2:7–8). This response must be demonstrated in his "deeds": repentance and obedience are never reduced to mere decisions but must be supported by visible and measurable actions.

"There is no partiality with God" (2:11)—God does not spare Jews or condemn Gentiles simply because of who they are. Rather, He looks at the heart of each person—what he knows, what he does, and what his intentions are (Heb. 4:12–13)—and judges accordingly. It is true that some will have more advantage in this life than others; it is not true that such advantages (or even disadvantages) will force a certain outcome. Being a just and impartial Judge, God will take into consideration in all relevant factors (upbringing, education, influences, talents, limitations, etc.) regarding one's earthly situation.

Paul speaks directly and forcefully about God's "wrath" (2:5, 8). He will direct His divine anger at those who suppress His revealed truth (recall 1:18); who do not repent; who are "selfishly ambitious," "do not obey the truth," and "[do] evil" (2:5–9). On the other hand, those who persevere in "doing good" and seek "honor and immortality" through divine grace will fully experience God's glory and honor (2:7, 10).

Law Is a Moral Standard (2:12–16): For 1,500 years, the Law of Moses governed the Jews; Gentiles were under a different law (2:12–16).[52] Jews, being under the Law of Moses, would be judged by that Law; Gentiles, being under a different law, would be judged by whatever law they lived under. Jews either "live" (i.e., are justified) by their faithful obedience to the Law of Moses, or they will "perish" (i.e., be condemned) by their unfaithfulness to that Law (2:12). Gentiles, who are not under the Jews' Law, will nonetheless "live" or "perish" by a law which they *ought to have known*, based upon what has been "clearly seen, being understood through what has been made, so that they are without excuse" (Rom. 1:20). One's *deeds*, not merely his knowledge (of law), reveals his true obedience or disobedience (2:13).

Paul refers to a "law written in their [Gentiles'] hearts" (2:14-15), which requires the activity of the human "conscience."[53] But "law" and "conscience" really are two different things: "law" refers to the (knowledge of the) commandments themselves, while "conscience" refers to the moral governance that tells a person whether he is living in compliance with those commandments. "When the mind is at work weighing evidence and making arguments, etc., we call that 'reasoning' and when the mind renders a verdict on our conduct we call that 'conscience.' The conscience is the mind functioning as a judge!"[54] In some cases, one's conscience will accuse him of violating his knowledge of God's law; in other cases, his conscience will defend his actions as being consistent with that law. (One's conscience *can be mistaken* but still attempts to justify his behavior.)

All this begs several questions. First, what was the law by which the Gentiles were judged? Second, does that law still exist today? Third, will all those who are not under the (law of the) gospel of Christ nonetheless be judged by it? It must be stated up front that no explanation offered here will satisfy every Christian's inquiry into this profound subject. Moralists, philosophers, and theologians of every flavor have been grappling with these kinds of questions for centuries. However, consider a few prominent points:

❑ The Gentiles most certainly lived under a (for lack of better term) universal moral law. This law not only had to have been *known* to them, but they also had to make a conscious decision either to obey or disobey it. God cannot charge people with sin in the absence of law (Rom. 4:15, 5:13); the fact that God did charge the ancient Gentiles with sin necessarily implies the active presence (and His active enforcement) of law. This moral law is universal because it applies to *all* people, regardless of covenant status.

- This universal moral law was a binding requirement upon the ancients, regardless of whether it was codified (i.e., written out). For example, Cain knew it was wrong to murder his brother Abel without God having to spell it out for him in writing (Gen. 4:7-11). Cain could not be guilty of sin unless he violated (transgressed) a law by which he was held accountable to God. Likewise, all those who perished in the Flood had to *know* they were doing evil, but simply paid no attention to this knowledge (Gen. 6:5).
- God's divine nature serves as this universal moral law. Failure to conform to this serves as the basis for all sin. Once a person sins, he can only be justified by faith in God, no longer by obedience to law.
- All covenants made by God, whether with Jews or Gentiles, require the same *moral* laws, and thus the same moral conduct. Morality is a constant: rites, rituals, ceremonies, specific expectations, etc. may change between covenants, but morality itself never changes.
- The only covenant of salvation offered to people today is the gospel of Christ (John 14:6, Acts 4:12, 1 Tim. 2:3-6, etc.). This means that all those (of an accountable age) who are outside of Christ are judged by the universal moral law; all those who are "in Christ" are judged by the law of Christ. The *moral expectations* of both groups are the same, but those who are "in Christ" have far more responsibilities because of their covenant relationship with God.
- One who is outside of Christ—an unconverted sinner—is not bound to the gospel of Christ but to the universal moral law. A person cannot be bound to a covenant to which he never agreed to honor. Once a person is baptized into Christ, however, he agrees to the covenant terms and is bound to this covenant for the rest of his life. (This gets ahead of where we are at in *Romans* so far, but it clarifies the status of the two parties.)[55]

It is not Paul's point—or his responsibility—to expound upon the "law" by which the ancient Gentiles were judged. Paul's emphasis is that God is a fair and impartial Judge; therefore, He can justify the one who puts his faith in Him, regardless of what law he is under. God would be unfair and partial, however, if He judged a person according to a standard (law or covenant) that was unknown or did not apply to him.[56] As it is, God presides as a fair Judge over the souls of all people. "[A]ccording to my gospel" (2:16) does *not* mean that every man will be judged *by* the gospel, but that Paul's gospel spells out the state of being of every person, whether he is in Christ or not.[57] "[T]hrough Christ Jesus" indicates that all judgment has been given over to God's Son (John 5:22-30; see 2 Cor. 5:10). Just as all salvation comes through Christ, so all judgment comes through Him.

Jews Also Stand Guilty before God (2:17–29)

ALL IMPLICATIONS ASIDE, Paul now speaks to Jews in a broad, historical sense. Specifically, he has in mind those who "rely upon the Law [of Moses] and boast in [their covenant relationship with] God" (2:1, bracketed words are mine). Such men are not Jewish Christians but are those who put their confidence in law-keeping as a means of righteousness (see Rom. 10:2-4). Thus, "you" must refer to the Jews generally and not to members of the church in Rome—most of whom he does not even know.

The Jews Are Also Lawbreakers (2:17–24): Regardless, Paul does not deny the enlightenment a Jew might offer a Gentile (2:17–20); he merely states that this privilege by itself does not translate to righteousness. Even while observing the literal words of the commandment of the Law of Moses, the Jews had long violated the essence of what God had taught *through* the commandment. The OT is filled with enough historical evidence to support Paul's statements (see Rom. 10:21). The Gospels also offer sufficient testimony against the Jews. Jesus accused them of hypocrisy (Mat. 15:1–9, 23:13–36, etc.), not understanding the Scriptures (Mat. 22:29), and being in league with Satan (John 8:42–47).

The Jews were keepers and guardians of the Law of Moses—a fact they often and proudly paraded before the Gentiles—yet they could not be justified by that Law (Acts 13:38-39, 15:6-11). Their violation of the Law of Moses made them sinners just like Gentiles who violated God's moral law (2:21–23). Specifically, some Jews were guilty of theft (2:21), often by withholding from God what should have been given to Him (Mal. 3:8-9) or by withholding from their parents what the Law commanded (Mat. 15:4-6). Also, some Jews were guilty of adultery (2:22)—Jesus Himself called them "an evil and adulterous generation" (Mat. 12:39)—if not against their spouses, then against their covenant with God. And, while the Jews did not practice idolatry in the way that their forefathers did, they "robbed temples" [lit., committed sacrilege against holy things (of God)], again by withholding tithes and sacrifices from God, or by using temple donations for ungodly purposes.

In other words, the Jews boasted in being law-keepers when in fact (historically) they were lawbreakers, putting them in league with the Gentiles who did the same thing. Instead of boasting an empty boast, the Jews should have humbled their hearts and repented (recall 2:4), thus setting an excellent example for the Gentiles to follow in their (the Gentiles') pursuit of God's fellowship. Instead, they blasphemed [lit., profaned] God's name in their arrogance (2:24). Paul quotes from Isa. 52:5 to underscore this—in other words, this is not a new problem but a deeply entrenched one.

Circumcision of the Heart (2:25–29): The Jews also boasted in their circumcision [lit., cutting off the male foreskin], since this was distinctive of their covenant with God (Gen. 17:10–11, Lev. 12:1–3, etc.). Yet, Paul responds that their unfaithfulness to that covenant rendered their physical circumcision useless. In fact, the uncircumcised Gentile could be justified by his faith without circumcision. In other words, circumcision (which often was used to symbolize obedience to the entire Law) was not the source of righteousness but faith. The Gentile whom God justified because of his faith in Him lived more like a genuine Israelite than the circumcised Jew who carelessly violated the Law. The Jew might be one "outwardly" because of his ethnicity, heritage, and physical conformity to the Law, but the Gentile's inward faith was what God sought all along (2:28).[58] True circumcision "is that which is of the heart, by the Spirit, not by the letter [of the Law]" (2:25–29). So it is today: true Christianity is not about religious rites and churchgoing but genuine faith in God for salvation. The Jews put great emphasis on the flesh;[59] God's emphasis in on the human heart.[60]

What Paul is really saying—and this reverberates throughout the entire epistle—is this: God has *always* justified people "by faith," not law-keeping. And inseparable from this, God has *always* justified people through divine grace (as a response to human faith), not law-keeping. No one can keep the laws of God perfectly, save Jesus Christ, so the only recourse the sinner has is "by grace…through faith" (Eph. 2:8). Faith is not a new subject that Paul introduces to the world but an ongoing one. The only thing that has changed is that *Christ* now needs to be the object of one's faith. It is the *heart* that needs to be circumcised *by* Christ, an action which is performed upon one's baptism into Him (Col. 2:11–12).

All Have Sinned and Are Guilty before God (3:1–20)

PAUL HAS THUS FAR MADE SOME EXTREMELY CONTROVERSIAL STATEMENTS, especially from a Jewish point-of-view. It might seem, then, that he favors Gentiles over Jews, or that he is justifying salvation to Gentiles at the Jews' expense. Anticipating these objections, Paul provides several rhetorical statements (both literal and implied) to clarify the position upon which he is expounding (3:1–8).

> **First:** "If a Jew is no better than a Gentile, what benefit is it to be a Jew?" (paraphrase of 3:1). Yet, Paul says, the Jew *does* have an advantage over the Gentile (3:2)—even though this advantage will not by itself *save* him. This also provides a springboard into the next point, namely, that God is faithful to the "oracles" which He entrusted to Israel.

> **Second:** "If some [Jews] did not believe, their unbelief will not nullify the faithfulness of God, will it?" (paraphrase of 3:3). Paul's point: the oracles (promises) of God concerning universal salvation were not dependent upon the faithfulness of the entire nation of Israel. Even as the people of Israel were sent into captivity for their sins, God remained faithful to His covenant with them (Lev. 26:40–45). If God were not faithful, then a person's faith in Him would be useless: God would act regardless, saving those whom He wanted to save and condemning those whom He wished to condemn.[61] God deals individually with every person according to what he has done (2 Cor. 5:10; cf. Ezekiel 18:20); the promises He makes to one person are not nullified by the faithlessness of another. Even if every person were a liar, God will never lie or default on His promises (2 Tim. 2:13, Titus 1:2).

> **Third:** "If God is shown to be faithful despite men's unfaithfulness, then why is God angry with men—especially the Jews?" (paraphrase of 3:5). Paul anticipates a Jew proposing the following conundrum: "Although we [Jews] put the Messiah to death, this is exactly what God wanted and expected us to do for the benefit of all mankind. How then can He find fault with us?"[62] But Paul argues that God judges according to the crime; what He does in response to (or because of) the crime is a different matter altogether. This would be like God thanking the serpent for deceiving Adam and Eve so that Christ could offer His gospel of

salvation! The gift of grace is never a license to sin, nor does it condone sinning to bring about more grace. It is one's own transgression that condemns him, not God alone. God only finalizes (in judgment) what each person has chosen in this life, whether it be "Light" or "darkness" (John 3:18–21). God never takes responsibility for our sins; rather, He provides divine remedy (atonement) for sinners.

Fourth: "If the gospel glorifies God by highlighting the disobedience of men, then is God fair to condemn men whose sins actually magnify God's grace?" (paraphrase of 3:7). The reality is just the opposite: one's sin dishonors God (recall 2:24), so that the result (saving grace) does not justify the means (human sin). Furthermore, God is glorified only when sinners choose obedience over disobedience, not the other way around. "The Jew should have remembered that God is author to two classes of promises. In the one he proposes to bless Israel, provided they keep his statutes. In the other, he threatens to punish, if they do not."[63]

Fifth: "If sin glorifies God, then let us sin often!" (paraphrase of 3:8). This maligns what Paul preached, yet some accused him of saying it. God never endorses (directly or indirectly) men who act irresponsibly or immorally. Evil is never good (Isa. 5:20); even a so-called "lesser of two evils" is still evil. Those who think otherwise have abandoned sound reasoning and show contempt for the divine nature of God, which is blasphemy. Thus, Paul is blunt in his response: "Their condemnation is just."

All People Are Guilty before God (3:9–20): "What then? Are we [Jews] better than they [Gentiles]? Not at all ..." (3:9). Paul now brings his argument to a climax (3:9–18): *all* who have sinned against *any* law of God are sinners, whether Gentiles (learned Greeks or barbaric heathens) or Jews (including ancient Israelites). God is faithful to all men—thus innocent of any injustice or sin—but all people have failed in every attempt at self-justification. Pulling together several OT quotes,[64] Paul paints a grim picture: despite great human accomplishments otherwise, all people are (morally and spiritually) fallen creatures. No person can remove the guilt of his sin or the damage it causes. "There is none righteous, not even one" (3:10)—this refers to a person's state of being apart from having been justified by God for his faith in God. Where Paul is leading with this discussion is clear: since all have sinned, therefore all need the grace of God. And grace will not work in the absence of human faith.

The Law of Moses was never meant to redeem sinners; it could not restore one's lost innocence before God (3:19–20).[65] Cold, unsympathetic, and inflexible law cannot save the one who sins against it. The only thing law can do is to justify the one who keeps it perfectly *or* condemn the one who violates it.[66] "Every mouth [is] closed [lit., silenced; stopped[67]]" means that no person has a right to speak in his defense, since every person stands guilty before God (see Rom. 11:32 and Gal. 3:22 for similar usage). Paul means here that "the argument for the depravity of the Jews from the Old Testament was so clear and satisfactory, that nothing could be alleged in reply. This may be regarded as the conclusion of his whole argument, and the expressions may refer not to the Jews only, but to all the world."[68]

Since God is our Creator, and we are His Creation, "all the world" is accountable to Him. He has sovereign authority over us; we must answer to that authority. He is the lawgiver—and we are all law-*breakers*—and He must enforce His law. Furthermore, "through the Law [or, through law] comes the knowledge of sin" (3:20): God has provided a code of righteousness, and anything that falls short of this is sin (Rom. 7:7–12, Gal. 3:19, etc.). Thus, we know (through His law) what both righteousness *and* sin look like.

We Are Justified by Grace through Faith (3:21–31)

Justification by Faith, Not Law (3:23–31): Against the backdrop of the hopelessness of our sinful state, Paul now provides the grand solution to it: Jesus Christ (3:21–26). This also marks a significant turning point in this epistle: while our sins separate us from God, Christ can reconcile us with God through Himself—that is, through Christ's own worthiness. God's righteousness is revealed *not* simply by the giving of law, but more importantly by providing a way of escape from law's condemnation (3:21–22). This was evident in the Law and the Prophets and is now evident in the gospel of Christ—i.e., "from faith to faith" (recall 1:17). (The "apart from law" phrase will be addressed in comments on 3:28.) God had showed saving grace to Israel whenever He forgave them of their sins against His law. However, the full explanation of *how* and *why* He was able to do this was not revealed until Christ appeared in the flesh and gave Himself as a once-for-all offering for sin.[69]

"[F]or all have sinned …" (3:23): every person who is accountable to God's law eventually *breaks* that law, incurring his own guilt. To "fall short of the glory [lit., holiness] of God" means to fail in one's moral obligation to keep what the Creator has established as a code of righteousness (i.e., God's holy nature).[70] The only way a sinner can be justified [lit., made innocent] before God is through His saving grace which comes by way of the blood of Christ. This grace is a "gift" because: it is not deserved; it cannot be earned; it cannot be purchased; it cannot be obtained through any other means. God imparts grace to "all those who believe" (3:22)—regardless of Jew or Gentile—through the blood of Christ (3:24–25). As a result of His sacrificial death on the cross, Christ redeems the believer's soul from law's condemnation (3:25). His blood provides "propitiation," meaning, the appeasement of God's wrath for our having sinned against Him. In this way He becomes the sinner's Advocate, and His blood cleanses the contrite sinner of his guilt (1 John 1:7, 9, and 2:1–2).[71]

Much could be said concerning Christ's sacrifice. Christ's sacrifice covers (atones for) all sins committed *prior* to it as well as all sins committed *after* it.[72] His death not only fulfilled the blood offerings of the Law of Moses, but also satisfied "once for all" what God required of the one who had sinned against Him (Heb. 5:9): that person's life. Blood is the essence of life (Lev. 17:10–11), the physical substance that links a person to his spiritual (non-physical) existence.[73] Christ's literal blood is the only physical antidote for one's spiritual fall from glory (Eph. 1:7); yet His blood necessarily required an uncorrupted body (Heb. 10:5–10). We are justified, then, by His body *and* His blood, for one is impossible without the other.

Paul's point: God is both *just* (or, righteous toward men) and the *justifier* (the determiner of the righteousness *of* men) (3:26). God never credits righteousness *apart* from one's faith but only when one *lives* by faith (recall 1:17: "the righteous man shall live by faith"). This need for divine grace nullifies all human boasting—in oneself, his law-keeping, or self-justification (3:27). One cannot boast in the very law he has broken, since that law can no longer justify him. No longer can his works save him but only his faith in God.[74]

A "law of faith" means here (3:27) a law that *defines what this faith must look like*, rather than each one defining "faith" on his own. If God justifies us by faith in Him, He also has the right and responsibility to reveal what this faith must be. We are thus "justified by faith apart from works of the Law"

(3:28).⁷⁵ The means of justification of the human soul lies outside of human effort, human works, or human ability. The best we can do is to keep the law of God; but once we fail—even once (James 2:10)—we are fully dependent upon *divine grace* to restore us to innocence. This is what "apart from" law means.⁷⁶ Law can only describe the situation at hand; it cannot rectify it once a person has become a lawbreaker. Divine grace *can* and *does* restore the human soul, but this is conditioned upon one's obedient faith. God's system of grace-through-faith functions equally with both Jew and Gentile (3:29–30). He does not justify one differently than He justifies the other; "there is no distinction between Jew and Greek; for the same Lord is Lord of all, abounding in riches for all who call on Him" (Rom. 10:12).

Paul then anticipates another objection, likely from a Jew (3:31), which we might paraphrase: "Does the teaching of the gospel to Gentiles nullify the Law of Moses given to the Jews?" Put another way: "Does being justified by faith nullify the need for law?" Paul responds confidently: "May it never be!" [KJV: "God forbid!"]. Such a thought violates the divine nature of God; no one can live in fellowship with God who will not keep His laws (1 John 2:4–6). Since justification by faith preceded the Law of Moses and even circumcision (as Paul explains in the next chapter), then it stands to reason that the Law cannot be in contradiction to this justification.

"On the contrary, we establish the Law"—lit., "we establish law," since there is no definite article ("the") before either use of "law" in this verse. The binding force of God's universal moral code of expected human behavior is upheld if, having violated that law, we must be justified by faith. In other words, the fact that we need faith (and a Justifier of it) underscores the fact that we are sinners, which necessarily implies that we have broken God's law, which necessarily implies that God's law *does exist*. In this way, "we establish [support; honor the standing of]" the existence of divine law when we seek redemption through faith. Law is not nullified but is necessary to define righteousness *and* transgressions (Gal. 3:19). If we were not lawbreakers, then neither would we need faith, grace, or justification.

Historical Examples of Justification by Faith (4:1–25)

Works Cannot Save Sinners (4:1–8): No person—save Christ—can be justified by law, since all fall short of the glory of God (recall 3:23). As a case in point, Paul cites one of the most respected men of all time (Abraham) to show that he was justified by faith, not perfect law-keeping (4:1–12; see Heb. 11:8–19). Abraham serves as an ideal representative here since he was the forefather of Gentiles (through Ishmael) as well as Jews (through Isaac). God "reckoned" or credited righteousness to Abraham because of his belief in Him, even though he had not yet seen what God had promised him (Gen. 15:6).[77]

If Abraham had been justified by works (i.e., if he had been a perfect man), then "he has something to boast about"—he would not need God's justification, for his perfect life would serve as the basis for fellowship with God. If he had been sinless, then he would have received his righteousness as earned "wages" (4:4) rather than having it bestowed upon him as a gift. As it was, Abraham was not a perfect man and thus required God's intervention (grace) based upon the confidence (faith) he put in Him (4:2–4). This reveals a great paradox: faith must have works to make it real, yet no one is justified *by* those works. A person's "faith [in God] is credited as righteousness [by God]" (4:5) once that faith is made real through appropriate action. No one who has sinned can be made righteous apart from God, and no one comes to God except through Christ (John 14:6).

Paul then introduces another man whom the Jews greatly respected (4:6–8): King David. David's sins are well-documented in Scripture; yet God forgave him of those sins.[78] God imparted this forgiveness because of His grace as the result of David's faith in Him. It was "apart from works" (4:6) in the sense that such forgiveness is not achieved through law-keeping (or human effort): David's sins made this impossible. God is the One who "credits" (or "reckons"; "imputes") righteousness; it is not bestowed through pious deeds, penance, religious authorities, churches, or the mere reading of Bible verses. In other words, divine action is required for a person to be forgiven (4:7–8; Paul quotes from Psalm 32:1–2, a psalm of David). Such action is in response to human faith and will not be imparted otherwise.

Faith Is Greater Than Circumcision (4:9–15): The Jews prided themselves on their circumcision, since this was a sign of the covenant given to them by God through Abraham (Gen. 17). Yet God credited Abraham with righteousness before he was circumcised; and God forgave David regardless of it (4:9–12; see John 8:39).[79] The system of justification by faith, then, precedes the Jews' boast in circumcision and is therefore superior to it. "Circumcision is nothing, and uncircumcision is nothing, but what matters is the keeping of the commandments of God" (1 Cor. 7:19). Believers demonstrate faith by keeping God's commandments (1 John 5:1–4), and without faith it is impossible to have fellowship with God (Heb. 11:6).

The Law of Moses was not the fulfillment of God's promises to Abraham (4:13; see Gen. 12:1–3 and Gal. 3:16–18). In other words, God did not rest the future blessing of "all the families of the earth" (Gen. 12:3) upon the Jews' law-keeping, but upon His own ability. The divine promise of blessing and salvation would be "nullified" (i.e., rendered useless) if it had been dependent upon every Jew's perfect law-keeping (4:14). Law "brings about wrath" (4:15)—i.e., God's codified laws which dictate right behavior condemn those who fail to live by them; the "wrath of God" is against all such unrighteousness (recall 1:18); such wrath implies impending punishment. If there was no law of God, there would be no standard by which to judge human behavior; one cannot be in violation of a law that does not exist (4:15). The fact that God charges people—*all* people, regardless of covenant status, even in the absence of it—with sin necessarily demands that they have violated His law.

Just as Abraham was justified by grace through his faith in God, so is every person today justified the same way (4:16; see Gal. 3:18 and Eph. 2:8). When we exhibit the same faith as Abraham, "the father of us all [who believe]," we become his descendants and are heirs of the divine promise (Rom. 9:8, Gal. 3:7, 29). This is implied in God having changed Abram's name to "Abraham," meaning, "a father of many nations" (4:17a, quoted from Gen. 17:5). We are not his descendants according to a physical lineage but according to a living faith.

In 4:17b–21, Paul includes an example of the kind of faith that Abraham demonstrated (see Gen. 17:15–19 and 18:1–14). Abraham was an old man (one hundred years) and Sarah, his wife, was an old woman (ninety years). Sarah's womb was, in a sense, doubly-dead: it was both barren and beyond child-bearing years. Yet, God promised Abraham a son through his wife, and Abraham believed that God could "[call] into being that which does not exist" (4:17b), just as he later believed that God could raise Isaac from the dead, if necessary (Heb. 11:17–19). Abraham believed "in hope against hope" (4:18)—that is, in hope *in the divine promise* against all hope *in human ability*.[80] He put his future entirely in God's hands and believed that He was able to perform where all human effort would fail (4:21).

The record of Abraham's faith serves as a model example for us (4:23–25). This *kind* of faith is what God requires to credit us with righteousness. First, one must believe that God is willing and able to perform beyond any human or natural effort. Second, one must demonstrate that faith in some visible and measurable way. Specifically, one must believe that Jesus resurrected from the dead and then live according to that belief (4:24; see Acts 17:30–31). Just as Abraham's own ability to fulfill God's promise was "dead" (Heb. 11:11–12), so we are "dead" to God without Christ (Eph. 2:1). Yet, just as God brought forth Abraham's son of promise (Isaac) from the deadness of Sarah's womb, so He brought Christ back from the dead and has "made us alive together with Christ" (Eph. 2:5–6).

Section Two: Benefits of Being Justified by Faith (5:1—8:39)

The Benefit of Peace with God (5:1–21)

Now Paul takes justification by faith to another level. Not only is the faithful believer credited with righteousness, but he also receives tremendous spiritual benefits. These benefits include peace with God (chapter 5); newness of life (chapter 6); freedom from condemnation (chapter 7); and the indwelling of the Holy Spirit (chapter 8).

Christ's Intercession for Sinners (5:1–11): "Therefore" (5:1) indicates that the conclusions Paul is about to draw build upon the foundation already laid in previous chapters. Notice the order (sequence) of the giving of these benefits (5:1–2):

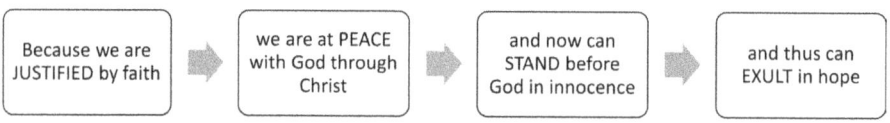

No one can "exult in hope" who does not "stand before God"[81]; no one can "stand" who is not "at peace with God"[82]; and no one has peace apart from being "justified." Faith is the catalyst for this justification: no one can seek God's favor without it (Heb. 11:6). Both faith and justification are objective in nature: faith needs to be *in* someone, and "justification" requires someone to *do* the justifying. The object of our faith is Jesus Christ (recall 3:23–26): He is the One in whom we must place our faith. The justifier is God, the only One in the position and having the authority to do this.[83]

"Peace with God" does not mean merely having a peaceful feeling, to be at peace with oneself, or imagining it into existence. Peace with God—like righteousness—is a real condition of the soul, not a mere sensation of the human conscience.[84] To be at peace with God requires unity with Him, which is only possible through His grace. This grace is possible only through the redemptive and intercessory work of "our Lord Jesus Christ" (5:1). The word "introduction" (5:2) comes from the same Greek word [*prosagoge*] which is also translated "access" (Eph. 2:18, 3:12): we have access to God when we live by faith in Him, but we stand before God because of His grace.

All of this is cause for exultation—i.e., glorying or boasting in God because of what He has done for the one who believes in Him (Rom. 15:17, 1 Cor. 1:30–31, 2 Cor. 10:17, etc.).

Those who are at peace with God can overcome this world (5:3–5). Paul explains the process of this overcoming:

- "**we exult in our tribulations**": This does not mean we are happy to endure these, but—having been justified—we can see their positive effect on our spiritual well-being (2 Cor. 12:10, James 1:2–4).[85] While the unconverted suffer without hope, believers suffer with a view to their redemption. Thus, we have peace amid tribulation, hope amid suffering, and can "exult" (or boast; rejoice) because of our spiritual standing with God.
- "**… perseverance**": This refers to the tenacity and determination to keep on keeping on, despite discouragements and struggles. Christians do not live in an idyllic vacuum, untouched by threats, nagging doubts, or assaults on our faith. Yet, we can endure these because of the One who justifies us (Luke 21:19, Heb. 10:36).
- "**… proven character**": This refers to a "tried condition" in which something (or someone) is put to the test.[86] God allows (and provides opportunities) for our faith to be "tested," since an untested faith really is no faith at all (1 Peter 1:6–9). Words alone do not produce proven character; it is earned only when one goes through the crucible of trials with his faith intact.
- "**… hope**": The Christian's hope is based upon the authority of Jesus Christ and His proven worthiness (2 Tim. 2:11–13). The Holy Spirit is "given to us"—the context here has nothing to do with miracles (as in Acts 8:14–17) but what is done for every person in whom the love of God has been "poured out," resulting in salvation (recall 8:6–9).

Paul then emphasizes how great our justification really is by magnifying what God did to secure it. This passage (5:6–11) is one of the finest summations of the gospel of Christ in the NT. First, Paul reveals the awful situation of those condemned because of sin. They are:

- "**helpless**" (**5:6**). Sinners cannot help themselves, nor can anyone else rescue them from their state of condemnation. This will a require a literal act of God.
- "**ungodly**" (**5:6**): Their sins having separated them from God (Isa. 59:1–2, Eph. 2:1–3), those who are unsaved are without providential guidance or influence.

- ❏ **"sinners" (5:8):** While this seems obvious, it is necessary to underscore the point. A "sinner" (here) is not merely one who has committed a sin but practices it; likewise, one who is righteous is not merely one who does a single righteous deed but practices righteousness (1 John 3:4–10).[87] Outside of Christ, all people practice sin—regardless of the kind, quantity, or frequency of those sins.
- ❏ **under divine wrath (5:9):** This point has already been made (recall 1:18–20 and 2:8) but needs re-emphasized. The sinner is an object of God's righteous anger: God is not merely displeased or unhappy with him but will unleash His *fury* against him for his having defied his Creator—unless that person is cleansed of his sins.
- ❏ **"enemies" (5:10):** As in the case of all idolatry, we take on the character of whatever we worship. One who befriends the godless world takes on that world's hostile character and therefore becomes God's enemy (James 4:4). Such people are worthy of death (cf. Luke 19:27). No one can hope to enter God's eternal fellowship who remains His enemy and refuses to seek reconciliation with Him.

This paints a bleak and frightening picture. Those who are outside of Christ (i.e., not "in Christ") are in a realm of spiritual darkness from which they cannot escape; this is what it means to be "lost" (as in Luke 15:24, 19:10).[88] While still on earth, sinners do not experience the full effect of what this means; often, they are altogether oblivious to the problem. They gospel of Christ is "veiled" to them; they are "blinded" by satanic influences and godless activity (2 Cor. 4:3–4). Yet, once they leave this earth, they will immediately be confronted with the reality of their awful situation—but then it will be too late.

While a person remains alive *there is hope*, but he finds his hope only in Jesus Christ. God sent His Son to save us from our horrible predicament "at the right time" (5:6). Throughout Scripture, God's plans are enacted *sequentially* and/or *conditionally*. This means: His plans are laid out by sequence (first this, then the next thing, then the next, etc.); *and/or* they are based on certain conditions (factors; optimal timing; ideal circumstances; etc.) being met. In the case of Christ's birth, ministry, and death, *both* apply. These followed a proper sequence of historical events *and* were the optimal timing of all things considered. He died "when the fullness of the time" came (Gal. 4:4) and only God could know what and when this "fullness" would be.

"Christ died for the ungodly" (5:6)—while "sinners" incur a death sentence, Christ provides *His* death as a satisfaction of (or propitiation for) this sentence (see 1 Peter 2:24). While someone might die for what that person believes is a "good man," Christ died for an untold number of *very bad people*—all enemies of God (5:7–8). The fact that He was willing to save us when we were at our worst magnifies His great love for us.

Christ's blood serves as the physical agent of atonement by which we are "justified" (5:9). This alludes to blood sacrifices required by the Law of Moses: when an Israelite offered such a sacrifice, God forgave him of his sins. Now, a far superior, "once for all" sacrifice has been offered to cleanse the soul of every believer who calls upon the name of the Lord for salvation. Animal blood could never remove sins (Heb. 10:1–10), yet everyone *is* justified (made innocent) through the blood of Christ (Eph. 1:7). Blood represents life (Lev. 17:10–11): in having been justified by Christ's blood, we are in fact justified by His *life* (1 Peter 3:18).

We enter God's fellowship through Christ (5:10). "Reconciliation" literally means "being made friends with again"—and thus no longer enemies.[89] This necessarily implies a previous good standing: one cannot be reconciled to a stranger, or to one from whom he has never been severed.[90] Since Jesus is no longer dead, but now reigns as our High Priest (Heb. 8:1), we are doubly saved: not only through His death but especially through His life, in the sense that He has been raised *from* His death and now mediates for us (5:10; see 1 Tim. 2:4–5 and Heb. 4:14–16).

Contrast of Christ's Gift and Adam's Fall (5:12–21): This section is admittedly difficult, partly because of the erroneous religious teaching that has been based upon it—namely, the so-called Doctrine of Original Sin— and partly because of the complex grammatical construction.[91] It helps to clarify the passage if one regards 5:13–17 as a parenthetical statement (which it is) and then reads 5:18 immediately following 5:12, as you see below:

> Therefore, just as through one man sin entered into the world, and death through sin, and so death spread to all men, because all sinned ... so then as through one transgression there resulted condemnation to all men, even so through one act of righteousness there resulted justification of life to all men.

In this section, too, Paul leaves all the "we" references behind and speaks objectively and with a view toward the entire history of all humankind. This is necessary and appropriate, given the universal scope of the doctrine upon which he expounds: he no longer refers only to how Christians have benefited from what God has done, but what God has done for all people. This supports his earlier-stated thesis: "For in it [the gospel] the righteousness of God is revealed from faith to faith" (recall 1:17)—and from generation to generation, even from covenant to covenant.

"Adam" refers to the man himself, the progenitor of humanity (5:12; see Gen. 5:1–2). Though it was Eve who sinned first (Gen. 3:1–6, 1 Tim. 2:14), it was Adam who bears the ultimate responsibility for bringing sin into the family, so to speak.[92] It was to him first and foremost that the commandment concerning the forbidden fruit was given. His violation of that commandment affects all those who come after him—thus, the entire human race. Through the very first human, "sin entered the world" and "death" was the curse for this (Gen. 2:16–17, Ezek. 18:4, Rom. 6:23, etc.). Consequentially, "death spread to all men" in a twofold sense:

- **First:** since the entire family of man is under a curse, all who are in that family will suffer its effects. This is true regardless of one's spiritual standing with God: even innocent children will suffer under this curse. To clarify: all will suffer the *effects* or *consequences* of sin in the world, but *guilt* is a far different matter.[93] Nowhere in Paul's writings—or anywhere in the NT—does it say that anyone is born guilty of another person's sin. Each person bears his own guilt when he sins against God. Paul's language is specific: "*…because all sinned*" (5:12, emphasis added). The personal consequence for sin only came to *those who sinned* (i.e., violators of God's law), not merely for being born into a sinful family.[94] This is not a new thought: "Fathers shall not be put to death for their sons, nor shall sons be put to death for their fathers; *everyone shall be put to death for his own sin*" (Deut. 24:16, emphasis added; see also Ezek. 18:20).
- **Second:** since sin is in the family (of man), each member of the family has the propensity or inclination to sin—and thus *will* sin eventually.[95] Adam's personal sin representatively communicates what will happen to all his posterity in due time. Just as Christ represents us all in receiving the opportunity for life in His name, so Adam represents us all in receiving the opportunity for death in *his* name, even if we do not commit the exact same error that he did.

In a parenthetical excursion from the thought he just began, Paul takes a moment to clarify some things (5:13–17):

- "sin was in the world" even before the Law of Moses defined, codified, and magnified its presence. If Adam (who lived long before the Law) was guilty of sin, he must have been under a law (5:13): the charge of sin demands the existence of law (recall 4:15). While the Law was given specifically to Israel (Psalm 147:19–20), a universal moral law existed for *all* people and was to have been obeyed.
- "from Adam until Moses" humankind still sinned against God and suffered under the curse of sin (5:14). Any violation of God's law resulted in the same condemnation (James 2:10). Adam serves as a "type" [Greek, *tupos*; lit., an impressed image; fig., a forerunner or prefigure] of Christ: the two are necessarily related in several ways, but the One (Christ) is also markedly superior to the other (Adam).
- "free gift" (5:15–17) recalls 3:24: "[We are] justified as a gift by His grace through the redemption which is in Christ Jesus." The "gift" is God's saving grace, which is everything He does to save us that we are unable to do. Specifically, this grace is personified in Christ Himself (Titus 2:11, 3:4–5). "But the free gift [of God] is not like the transgression [of Adam]"—in several ways:

Adam's Transgression	Christ's "Free Gift"
came through a man	came through the Son of God
was the result of temptation	was the result of perfect obedience
incurred divine condemnation	provides divine forgiveness
many "died" (were cursed)	many live (the curse is overcome)[96]
leads to many transgressions	leads to justification
many are made sinners (when they sin, following in the footsteps of Adam)	many are made righteous (when they believe in God, following in the footsteps of Christ)

- Since death is the payment (wage) for sin (Rom. 6:23), the effect of sin is not a "gift" but a horrible consequence (5:15). Grace, however, is not a "consequence" of faith but is gifted to those who seek God's fellowship. Sin only brings death and nothing else, but Christ brings a life overflowing with manifold blessings and advantages. In other words, it is not simply an exchange of "life" for "death." Rather, the two results are entirely disproportionate: "the free gift is not like [or not even comparable to—MY WORDS] the transgression."[97]

- In 5:16, Paul inverts the effects of one man (Adam) against the other (Christ). In Adam's case, *one sin* led to "many transgressions"; in Christ, these many transgressions are removed through the righteousness of *one life* (Christ's). While Adam's sin began a chain of events that negatively affected all human history, Christ's righteous life breaks that chain and gives fellowship with God in the place of condemnation.[98]

Paul picks up in 5:18 where he left off in 5:12 and continues to show the contrasts between the "first" Adam and the "second" Adam (i.e., Christ; see 1 Cor. 15:22). "The Law came in so that the transgression would increase" (5:20): the Law of Moses magnified the presence of sin and its ruinous effects (Gal. 3:19). God's laws reveal not only how sinful people really are but also how holy God is—and how sin severs people from God's holy fellowship. Law also magnifies the desperate human need for divine help in restoration to God's fellowship. Law itself cannot do this (Acts 13:38–39, Heb. 10:1–4); more laws or more dependence on law-keeping is not the answer. "The human race therefore did not receive help and healing from the Law [or law], but only an increase of its sickness [i.e., its awareness of sin]."[99] The more people sinned, the more they would need God's saving grace; "where sin increased, grace abounded all the more" (5:20).

The Benefit of Newness of Life (6:1–23)

Paul anticipates a rebuttal to what he just said concerning the increase of grace because of the increase of sin (6:1): the abundance of grace may encourage the practice of sin (6:1). This reasoning, of course, is illogical: God never promotes evil to bring about good; He never condones sin to impart grace. The practice of sin is incompatible with the practice of righteousness (1 John 3:4–10). Thus, Paul's strong response: "May it never be!" (6:2a).

One who has died to his allegiance to sin cannot still put himself under sin's control (6:2b). Death severs one's allegiance to his master, regardless of whether it is the death of the master or that of the servant (as in the sinner's case). The action that symbolizes our death to sin's reign (recall 5:21) and our new allegiance to Christ is baptism—immersion in water (6:3).[100] In other words, sin does not die to us, but we die to sin; sin continues to reign over other people, but (once we are baptized) Christ reigns over us.[101] Being "baptized into Christ" makes one a member of Christ's spiritual body (His church), providing access to God's fellowship.[102]

Walking in Newness of Life (6:3–11): Baptism symbolizes one's death, burial, and resurrection to "newness of life" (6:3–4). Just because baptism is symbolic does not make it optional, expendable, or unnecessary. The Passover celebration was hugely symbolic, yet God commanded the Israelites to observe it.[103] Many denominational teachers today reject the necessity of baptism for salvation, stating that it is merely "an outward sign of an inward grace" (Calvinism).[104] In other words, salvation has already occurred (but when?) and baptism simply provides a public witness to it. The NT simply does not teach this, but people do.

Christ died on the cross, was buried in the earth, and rose from the dead. His "old" life on earth ended (John 19:30); "behold, new things have come" (2 Cor. 5:17). Likewise, the believer[105] also "dies" to his "old" self, is buried in a watery grave,[106] and is resurrected to serve a new Master. The believer's actions are symbolic *of* Christ's literal death, burial, and resurrection. Both deaths are real but not equal: ours follows in form, not in significance. Nonetheless, through this act of faith:

- The believer is baptized into Christ (i.e., His body, the church—Col. 1:18).
- He is baptized into His death (i.e., he chose what Jesus chose). We tend to think, "We are imitating Christ's actions, thereby identifying with Him"—which is true, but limited. Beyond this, we are joining with Christ's *cause*—the *reason* for His death, to condemn sin in the flesh (see Rom. 8:3)—and accepting the losses and sacrifices that come with joining this cause (Mat. 16:24).
- One who is not baptized into Christ's death has not died with Him (2 Tim. 2:11).
- One cannot be "raised…to walk in newness of life" (6:4) who has not died with Christ and been buried with Him (in baptism).[107]
- We follow Christ when we obey His commands (John 14:15). Yet, one cannot obey a command to be baptized by refusing it (Mat. 28:19, Acts 2:38, 10:48, 22:16, etc.).

- Paul himself was baptized to "[call] upon the name of the Lord" (Acts 22:16; notice also the "us" of 6:3). If baptism is necessary to "call" upon the Lord for salvation, then to *refuse* to be baptized (for any reason) will not call for God's saving help.
- Baptism is when the believer is "born again" (John 3:5, 1 Peter 1:3) or "born of God" (John 1:12–13). It is inexplicable how one can be "born of God" without doing what God requires for this—and without *dying first* (in baptism).
- In baptism, one's "body of sin" is "done away with" since he submits to the God-given process to accomplish this (6:6). From this point forward, that person's allegiance is to be with Christ, no longer to sin (6:6–7).[108]
- "For all of you who were baptized into Christ have clothed yourselves with Christ" (Gal. 3:27): baptism is the historical and visible event that marks our spiritual transition from the world to Christ's church (Col. 1:13–14). It is the point of reference with which our full allegiance to Christ begins. There is only "one baptism" that God requires (Eph. 4:5): that which is done in faithful obedience to the gospel's commands.

The one who has died *with* Christ now belongs *to* Him (6:7). This implies a spiritual transaction: God purchases that person's soul through the blood of Christ; he no longer belongs to himself but is God's possession (1 Cor. 6:19–20, Titus 2:14). Christ, and no longer sin, reigns over him (6:7); he walks by the Spirit of God (Gal. 5:16–17), not according to the way of the world (or "flesh"). Just as he is not "partially" buried in water but fully immersed, so he is not "partially" dead to sin but fully. Having been "united with [Christ] in the likeness of His death" (6:5),[109] "we shall also live with Him" in the likeness of His glory (6:8; see Phil. 3:20–21 and 1 John 3:2). Just as Christ will never die again, so the believer's soul will never die; death is no longer "master" over him—it has no "victory" or "sting" as before (1 Cor. 15:54–57). Being "freed from sin" (6:7) does not mean (and cannot mean) that he will never sin again; it means that once he was a servant of sin, but now he is a servant of the Lord. Salvation is always a conditional promise ("*If* we have died with Christ…"—6:8; "*if* indeed you continue in the faith firmly established and steadfast, and not moved away from the hope of the gospel that you have heard"—Col. 1:23; *if* we confess our sins, He is faithful and righteous to forgive us our sins … —1 John 1:9; etc.). Unless the premise is met, the promise will be nullified.

As Christ died to (the world of) sin "once for all," so the Christian has died to sin once for all (6:10; see Heb. 10:10, 14). That which "once for all" completed will never need to be done again. Thus, there is no unfinished business on God's part regarding the salvation of human souls.[110] The subject here is not perfect or flawless obedience on our part but faithful *allegiance*. Even the most faithful Christian will still sin, but he will not abandon his allegiance to Christ (see 1 John 1:5—2:2). This is what it means to be "dead to sin, but alive to God in Christ Jesus" (6:11).

A New Allegiance to a New Master (6:12–23): Having defined the process by which one is justified to God, Paul now makes practical use of this transaction (6:12-23). Since the Christian is no longer a servant of sin, the "members of your body"—i.e., one's physical body—can no longer participate in sinful action.[111] Just as one's heart belongs to Christ, so also does his body: this must submit to the same God who has given life to his spirit. Therefore, one's body is now for the purpose of righteousness, in conformity with the One who sanctifies him (1 Thess. 4:7, 1 Peter 1:15, etc.). We can only imagine the impact of these words upon a people (in Rome) who once regularly indulged in carnal lusts, sexual immoralities, prostitution, and other sins of the body (cf. 1 Cor. 6:9-11, 1 Peter 4:1-3, etc.). It is incompatible with the gospel—and one's baptism—to practice sin while claiming to be a Christian.

Paul further explains: a Christian is "not under law but under grace" (6:14)—that is, he is no longer condemned by law (as a lawbreaker) but is justified by grace through his faith in the Justifier (recall 3:26; see Eph. 2:8, Titus 3:7, etc.). Paul's words here are misrepresented by some to mean, "You no longer have to obey commandments because you are always covered by grace." This contradicts what he said, not only here but in all his epistles. God will never permit, condone, or enable sin simply because of the availability of grace—Paul once again condemns such a thought (6:15; recall 6:1-2). It is impossible to remain true to the gospel of Christ by purposely avoiding any of God's commandments.

Rather than absolving us of our responsibility to law, "under grace" should in fact make us even more responsible to it. God's laws are not ornamental fixtures of His gospel but provide the structure for what it means to walk with Him. This refutes antinomianism [*anti-* (against) + *nomos* (law)], a human doctrine which assumes that since we are saved by grace, we are no longer accountable to law. This implies a "once saved, always saved" scenario (as Calvinism teaches): since one is "*under* grace" he can no longer fall *from* it. Paul does not teach this, but just the opposite (Gal. 5:1-4).

Christians—those baptized into Christ—are still servants, but we are servants to *God,* not sin (6:16-18). Servitude here necessarily implies obedience, and obedience to God is impossible apart from honoring His laws. A genuine expression of love for Christ requires obedience to His commands (see John 14:15, 1 John 2:4-6, and 5:2-3). Every person, Paul implies, serves *someone* or *something,* whether it be God or another master. Servitude to sin leads to death; servitude to God leads to righteousness (6:16).

The Roman Christians did not just stumble into obedience, servitude to God, or Christianity in general. They *learned* of these things through preachers of the gospel. Salvation is not something that happens to a person without his knowledge or consent (as Calvinism teaches). It is a *decision* of the believer based upon "that form of teaching" (6:17)—or "the doctrine conforming to godliness" (1 Tim. 6:3)—that he learned from God's word (see Eph. 1:13-14, Col. 1:5). This "form of teaching" necessarily implies a *revealed pattern of instruction* given by God so we can know "the will of the Lord" (Eph. 5:17).[112] One cannot be a "slave of righteousness" (6:18) who refuses—for any reason—this "form of teaching."

Paul admits that his "slaves to righteousness" analogy is a primitive one ("I am speaking in human terms because of the weakness of your flesh"—6:19). Even so, through Paul's analogy we can understand the change of allegiance—and form of obedience—that occurs upon one's having been justified by his faith. Paul sets the two allegiances in contrast (6:19-23):

Living under Moral Law	Justified by God	Living under Grace
Innocent, until a single violation of law	⟹	Made innocent, through the perfect obedience of Christ
Once having sinned, are condemned by God	⟹	Once having been justified, are reconciled to God
… are now slaves to sin	⟹	… are now servants of God
Disobedience continues, without any recourse	⟹	Righteousness continues as faith continues

Living under Moral Law	Justified by God	Living under Grace
Derive no benefit from sin	⟹	Derive tremendous benefits from God's mercy and grace
"the wages of sin is death"	⟹	"the free gift of God is eternal life in Christ" (6:23)

What benefit does one derive from an allegiance to sin? Paul says bluntly: there is none. Sin is inherently destructive, corrosive, and debilitating; it produces nothing but sorrow, shame, and ruin. Those enslaved to sin are "free [as in, unaffected or uninfluenced—MY WORDS] in regard to righteousness" (6:20). "For the outcome of those things [which you used to practice—MY WORDS] is death" (6:21): while the NT does not use the phrase "spiritual death," this is what is meant here. This does not refer to a soul's annihilation—a teaching foreign to the NT—but a permanent separation from God (Eph. 2:1–3).

"But now…" (6:22)—for the one who is "in Christ," *things have been radically and indescribably improved.* Instead of an eternal death (separation from God), the faithful believer can now look forward to "eternal life." This is not the result of human works, since no one who has sinned against God can any longer be justified by these; it is God's grace which provides "sanctification." To be sanctified means to be set apart for God's use, to be made holy to Him. Those who are sanctified are called, appropriately, "saints" (as in 1 Cor. 1:2).

The only thing the sinner earns, ironically, is his own spiritual death (6:23). He does not earn salvation because this is a "gift," never a wage (recall 3:24). To receive "the free gift of God" is the finest outcome any human soul could ever hope to have: an eternity spent with a benevolent God.

The Benefit of Freedom from Law's Condemnation (7:1–25)

Death Severs Earthly Allegiances (7:1–6): In this chapter, Paul continues the thought he began in 1:16, but particularly in 5:20. (Chapter breaks and the assignment of verses came about 1,500 years after this epistle was written.) One's severance from his allegiance to sin—and his subsequent allegiance to Christ—is analogous to being legally unbound (or freed) from a marriage. Paul speaks to those familiar with "the law" (7:1)—we assume this means the Law of Moses, but laws concerning marriage extended well beyond the ancient Israelites. It seems, then, that Paul speaks to those familiar with the law of *marriage*, which God implicitly ordained "from the beginning" (Mat. 19:4–6).

The law of marriage only has "jurisdiction" [lit., rule or dominion] over those who are living and are in a legal union; it cannot rule over those who are dead or not married. If a wife's husband dies, then she is no longer married to him, since death effectively and permanently severs that union (7:2). However, if a man's wife leaves him (while he is still living) to become another man's wife, "she shall be called an adulteress"—one who has illegitimately violated her lawful marriage.[113] However, if her husband dies, then she is free (i.e., unrestrained by law regarding the previous union) to become another man's wife (cf. Deut. 24:1–2). In this case, her first marriage no longer exists and is no longer functional; that relationship has ended (7:3).

"Therefore" (7:4) implies a conclusion drawn from what has just been said: death severs that which once bound one person to another. The institution of marriage does not die, but one can be dead to the institution (Mat. 22:30). Thus, "you [Christian] also were made to die" to the condemnation brought about by law (7:4). Once again, the condemnation of law did not die—it continues to condemn all other lawbreakers—but the believer died to its condemnation. The marriage illustration, then, is analogous but not perfect: in the illustration, the husband dies, liberating his wife from that which bound them together; here, it is (in effect) the *dead husband* who is liberated from his living wife. What is common between the two—and this is Paul's point—is that the death of one relationship makes possible the creation of a new relationship. Just as laws concerning marriage only have jurisdiction over those who are living and married, so the jurisdiction of law only exists if we are living in sin and thus condemned by the law that defines that sin.

This "death" is real, but not literal: we do not literally die to become joined to Christ in a new union. But we *must* "die" to sever sin's mastery over us; our baptism symbolizes this death (recall 6:3–7). Even so, someone did in fact die—one whose actual death validates our symbolic death. This was Christ's role: His literal death on the cross makes possible our symbolic death in baptism. He died not *instead* of us (because we must also "die," and our literal death could not have accomplished anything) but *for* us. Therefore, Paul says, "You also were made to die to the Law *through the body of Christ*" (7:4, emphasis added). Through His death, we are freed from law's condemnation (since His death fulfilled the penalty of that condemnation), and thus we can be legally bound to Christ instead. We are not bound to a dead man—a relationship which could not function—but to a Living Savior, "to Him who was raised from the dead."

Paul's use of "in the flesh" (7:5) indicates the context of one's allegiance rather than a physical state of being. "Flesh" here refers to the worldly disposition of an unconverted person, one whose heart is dictated by self-serving pleasures rather than his service to Christ. By indulging in these carnal pleasures, a person cannot "bear fruit" for God but only bears "fruit for death"—i.e., the unproductive results of a godless life (like "dead works" of Heb. 9:14). However, once a person is joined to the Lord (1 Cor. 6:17), he can bear much "fruit" because of the Spirit of God who indwells him. The Spirit "gives life" to our souls and good works that we produce (John 6:63, 12:24, 15:1–6, Gal. 5:22–23), as we will see in chapter 8. Likewise, the "newness of the Spirit"—our spiritual renewal brought about by the regeneration of the Holy Spirit (Titus 3:5)—contrasts with the "oldness of the letter" which offers no life but produces only death (7:6).[114]

God's Law, Though It Condemns, Is Just (7:7–13): Paul now anticipates another rebuttal, particularly from a Jew: "Since you claim that we need to be released from Law [of Moses], then you insinuate that the Law itself was problematic, even unjust—and that cannot be!" (paraphrase of 7:7). Paul responds in strong language: "May it never be!" God does not give defective or unjust laws; rather, His laws lead the human soul to life (Lev. 18:5, Luke 10:25–28). The purpose of God's codified laws was never to create problems but to magnify people's utter sinfulness and God's absolute holiness. Since a person cannot be justified by works of law, he must seek justification through his faith in God's grace.[115] The Law magnified the problem; it did not create it, but it could not solve it, either.

Paul draws upon his own experience as an example of what he means (7:7–13). Before understanding what coveting was, Paul considered himself "alive" (i.e., innocent; in God's favor). But when he learned the Law's teaching on coveting, it (the Law) revealed coveting within his own heart.[116] Instead of standing favorably before God, he realized that he fell short of God's glory (recall 3:23); upon that realization, "sin became alive and I died" (7:9). In other words, Paul could no longer claim to be innocent once he allowed sin to exercise mastery over him.

The commandment that exposed Paul's sin did not make the commandment itself sinful. The Law did not deceive Paul but enlightened him; sin is what deceived him—really, that blinded him to his true condition (cf. John 9:39–41). It was not the Law that "killed" Paul but sin (1 Cor. 15:56): because of sin, the law which once justified Paul's innocence now condemned him as a lawbreaker. "So then," he concludes, God's law is not at fault but rather the one who violates it. Paul did not hold God's law in contempt, but fully supported it: "the Law is holy, and the commandment is holy and righteous and good" (7:12).[117] The commandment of law declared sin to be "utterly sinful"—the cause of death to the human soul (7:13; recall 6:23).

The Struggle between One's Spirit and His Carnal Desires (7:14–25): This next section (7:14–25) explains why the Law (or simply, "law") is good and just, while the inclination of man's "flesh" is to pursue sin. This section is difficult for two reasons: first, the grammatical construction, though sound, is difficult to follow; second, there are disagreements over exactly what spiritual condition it is that Paul describes. Some believe he is describing himself (or any Jew who was under the Law of Moses) before becoming a Christian; others believe that Paul describes his state of mind after having become a Christian. Still others believe that Paul speaks of a godless heathen's state of mind before his conversion to the Lord.

Certain expressions ("sold into bondage to sin" or "body of this death") are inconsistent with the Christian's state of being (or Paul's pious attitude; see Phil. 3:3–6) but are appropriate for one who is not in Christ. Yet, he cannot be describing the state of mind of a godless heathen, either, since the one whom Paul describes "joyfully concur[s] with the law of God" in his heart (7:22).[118] It is true that the struggle between good and evil does not evaporate once a person becomes a Christian; in fact, in many ways that struggle is intensified. But if one reads this section from the point-of-view of a pious Pharisee—as Paul most certainly had been—it should become clear that he speaks retrospectively, not presently. Granted, the present tense in which he narrates this ("I am …"; "I do …"; etc.) seems to undermine this at first. Yet we do the same thing when we narrate in the present tense that which had happened in the past: "Okay, so I am going out to my car, and I see this guy standing there, and he hands me this brochure, etc." Besides, Paul's intention here is to support the holiness of "the Law" (7:12–13)—in this case, the Law of Moses—and he wrote this section with that support in mind.

The essential points of this passage:

- We cannot dismiss Paul's own involvement in his explanation. Just as he used himself as an example concerning coveting (7:7ff), so he continues to draw on his own experiences here. In other words, Paul is not speaking hypothetically but realistically and personally.
- Paul contrasts two sides of his own human nature: the "spiritual" man, which desires and delights in the laws of God; and his earthly nature, which desires to follow the impulses of the "flesh" (cf. 1 John 2:15–17).
- The laws of God compelled Paul to do what is good; his carnal desire—or simply "sin"—compelled him to pursue that which contradicts the laws of God. These two natures do not have peaceful coexistence but are antagonistic to each other (Gal. 5:16–17). "Sin is personified as an evil power which takes up its residence within human nature, and there controls man's actions."[119]
- Paul reveals an obvious struggle within himself while he was under the Law of Moses: he knew what was good yet did not always do it; he also knew what was evil yet, because of the law of God in his heart, he sought to avoid this (7:15–20). This was not a one-time battle but a continuous series of battles—in essence, an unseen *war* (7:23).
- Jesus said, "The spirit is willing, but the flesh is weak" (Mat. 26:41); Paul expresses the same principle in describing the conflicting natures within himself. While his heart was given over to God's law, he did not cease to be a carnal being who had once "sold [himself] into bondage of sin" (7:14).
- If left to his own carnal nature, Paul's own sinful passions would have consumed him—and this seems key to what he describes in 7:17–20. The laws of God, however, provide a positive reinforcement of the good behavior with which he so passionately serves the Lord (7:21–22). Thus, he rejoices over the benefits provided by these laws "in the inner man" (i.e., in his heart). This was true while he was a Pharisee, and it seems no less true now that he is a Christian.
- The "different law" (7:23) refers to that selfish human nature which rebels against God's laws and wages war against what is in Paul's heart

(see 1 Peter 2:11). "He says that sin produces a counterfeit law, which makes war upon the true law, takes man captive and so works its will with him."[120]

The point is: though he was a God-fearing, law-abiding Pharisee, Paul could not be justified by appealing to his own good conduct, for he admits here that his conduct was not always good. Having given in to the temptation of sin even once, he was no longer able to justify himself. However, he also admits that he (in that former state) was a seeker of God and longed for His fellowship.

"Wretched man that I am!" (7:24)—that is, if left in such a condition. "Who will set me free … ?"—a rhetorical question, since he has already defined Christ as the justifier of men's souls (Rom. 3:23–24). But he wishes to emphasize the great need for divine justification, for otherwise spiritual freedom is humanly impossible.

"So then …" (7:25)—to recap: Paul admits that, as a pious Pharisee, he was a spiritual being who deeply desired fellowship with God and was devoted to His law. However, he was also a carnal man who continued to fall short of God's glory. Paul cannot mean here, "Who will set me free from having to obey God's laws?" for it is impossible to define faith apart from obedience. He also cannot mean, "Who will set me free from my physical sinful body?" or "Who will set me free from ever having to struggle against sin again?" for such statements are unsupported by the context and are also unrealistic. What Paul is saying here seems to be, in essence: "How can I, a man who struggles against sin yet longs to live in God's favor, be justified before Him?" The answer—and there is only one answer (John 14:6)—is Jesus Christ.

The Benefit of the Spirit's Guidance (8:1–17)

Freedom from Law's Condemnation (8:1–4): Paul immediately addresses the rhetorical question he stated in 7:24: "Who will set me free from the body of this death?" He now states triumphantly, "There is now no condemnation for those who are in Christ Jesus" (8:1). "Now" is in sharp contrast to the implied "then" of his former experience as a pious Pharisee. "No condemnation" cannot mean that Christians are immune to sin or cannot fall from grace, since the Bible teaches otherwise (Acts 8:17–23, 2 Cor. 6:1–2, Gal. 2:11–14, 5:1–4, Heb. 6:4–8, 10:26–31, etc.). Rather, those "in Christ" are freed from the condemnation brought about by an unmerciful law. Law (by itself) is "sin and death" to us because the transgressor of law is guilty and cannot be redeemed except through divine grace. Lard writes, "'The law of the Spirit of life' I take to be a complex name for the gospel ... first, because it is a law in the truest sense of the word, ... and, secondly, because it is a rule of conduct."[121] The "law of ... Christ" (8:2) refers not only to commandments to be obeyed but encompasses the entire prescription for salvation ("of life"). Its source is God ("of the Spirit"), but the context in which it operates is "in Christ."

The believer's law is "of the Spirit" (from God), but the context in which it operates is "in Christ." God the Spirit provides sanctification (1 Peter 1:3) and access to God (Eph. 2:18) through His ministerial work. The Spirit's work is carried out in the individual believer as well as the collective body (church) of the saints.[122] To be "in Christ" means to be in a covenant relationship with God *through* Christ's intercession. One who is not "in Christ" is still in the world, under Satan's dominion, and condemned by God (Acts 26:15–18, Eph. 2:1–3, and Col. 1:13–14).

In describing the Law as "weak" (8:3), Paul only refers to what it was unable to do, not to any moral deficiency within it (Acts 13:38–39, Heb. 7:18). "[T]hrough the flesh" refers to the limitations of human ability to keep a divine law perfectly. To overcome this limitation required a *divine Personage* (Christ) to do what no ordinary human could do. Through His obedience, Christ proved Himself worthy to provide a sin offering to God on our behalf (Heb. 10:5–10). "[I]n the likeness of sinful flesh" refers to that which Christ represented, not something He became.[123] Though completely innocent of any crime (1 Peter 2:21), men condemned Him as a sinner (Mat. 26:65–66).[124]

In representing a sinner's death, Christ "condemned sin in the flesh" (8:3b): He proved that *every* sinner deserves to die. By sacrificing Himself *for* sinners, He robbed sin of its power *to* condemn them (see Heb. 2:14–15). The "requirement" of God's law (8:4a) is death to the one who violates it.

While Christ fulfilled this requirement on the cross, we participate in this requirement symbolically through our baptism into His death (recall 6:3–7).

Two "Walks" Contrasted (8:5–17): In 8:4b, Paul contrasts those "who do not walk according to the flesh, but according to the Spirit."[125] He takes the next several verses to expound upon this. To "walk" means to live in a certain way, with reference to one's regular habits; "flesh" here refers to the satanic spirit of worldliness, sensuality, and pride which stand in defiance of God's will (cf. Eph. 4:17–24, James 3:13–17, and 1 John 2:15–17). To walk "according to the Spirit" means to live in fellowship with God. Notice the contrasts between the two "walks" (8:6–17):

One Who Walks According to the Spirit:	One Who Walks According to the "Flesh":
Cannot walk according to the flesh	Cannot walk according to the Spirit
Sets his mind on things of the Spirit	Sets his mind on things of the flesh
Has life and peace in God (recall 5:1–2)	Is not at peace with God
Subjects himself to the will of God	Is in hostile opposition to God's will
Pleases God with his faithful obedience	Is unable to please God (Heb. 11:6)
Has the indwelling of the Spirit (1 John 4:13)	Does not belong to God and therefore does not have His Spirit indwelling him
His body is condemned to die, but his spirit is "alive because of righteousness"	His body *and* spirit are condemned
His body will be raised in glory by Christ "to a resurrection of life"	His body will be raised in shame "to a resurrection of judgment" (John 5:29)
Puts to death the deeds of the flesh	Indulges in deeds of the flesh (Gal. 5:19–21)
Is led by the Spirit of God	Is led by his self-serving lusts
Lives as a son (child) of God (Gal. 4:5–6)	Is enslaved by sin (John 8:34, Rom. 6:16)

As a legally adopted child of God, he has an inheritance from God (Eph. 1:9–11)	Since he has no relationship with God, is a stranger to Him without any inheritance
Will suffer in this life but glorified in the life to come (2 Cor. 4:16–18)	Will suffer in this life *and* in an eternal separation from God in the hereafter
Will live (John 6:40)	Will die (John 8:24)

The "mind" (8:6–7) refers to a person's will but is also identified in Scripture as one's "heart." The mind of an unconverted person seeks completion and gratification in the world; the mind of a Christian (ideally) seeks completion and fulfillment in Christ. To "set [one's] mind" on one or the other means to fixate one's attention on that which he believes will bring him the greatest advantage. The pursuit of human cravings leads to (spiritual) "death"; to walk by the Spirit leads to (spiritual) life (Gal. 5:16). One of the functions of the Holy Spirit is to impart life to God's creation: wherever is spiritual life is also the work of the Spirit.[126] One experiences "life and peace" who walks by the Spirit (8:6). Yet, one who walks opposed to God's Spirit is "hostile" to God: he makes himself God's enemy and therefore has no life in him (recall 5:10; see James 4:4). Such a "mind" (heart) "cannot please God" (8:8) because it operates in defiance of His will, His nature, and His commandments (1 John 1:5–10, 2:3–6).

"However" (8:9) indicates a contrast, but only when certain conditions are met (as implied by the several "if" statements). Being "in the Spirit" is synonymous with walking "according to the Spirit" (recall 8:4). These are mutually dependent states of being: one cannot walk according to the Spirit who is not in the Spirit; one who has God's Spirit must walk accordingly. Likewise, one who is indeed in the Holy Spirit must also be "in Christ" (recall 8:2) and Christ must abide in him (John 15:5–6); it cannot be otherwise.

Notice that Paul uses "Spirit of God" interchangeably with "Spirit of Christ" (8:9). These do not refer to two separate "Spirits," but one (Eph. 4:4).[127] The most natural explanation seems to be that the "Spirit of God" is a divine Personage that carries out God's will; this *same Spirit* also carries out Christ's will, which is always in agreement with God's, since both God and His Son are seamlessly united (John 10:30; 17:20–23). The same Spirit is both "of God" and "of Christ," in that He is the dynamic agent in conducting the divine work of the Godhead.[128]

The indwelling of the Spirit is spiritual in nature but is real all the same. The Spirit does not literally (or physically) indwell us anymore than sin can (recall 7:20); yet, as real as sin's presence is within the one who practices it, so the Spirit's presence is within the one who practices righteousness. When one's mind/heart is under the Spirit's influence, it necessarily follows that his physical body will also be given over to the Spirit's work. Thus, "Christians are men whose lives are directed from a source outside themselves."[129] It is not necessary that we fully understand how the Spirit indwells us to believe that He *does*, and that this indwelling produces necessary changes in the believer's life.

The human body, because it lives under the curse that God placed upon Adam (Gen. 3:17–19), is destined to die. It is in this sense that "the body is dead because of sin" (8:10). However, one's spirit can live to God even though his body will die. "The Spirit of Him who raised Jesus from the dead" (8:11) reveals that the Holy Spirit was directly involved in Jesus' resurrection from the dead; otherwise, there would be no reason to associate God's Spirit with that event. Paul alludes to Jesus' bodily resurrection, then anticipates our own (as in Phil. 3:10–11). "He who raised Christ Jesus from the dead"—both literally and bodily—"will also give life to your mortal bodies" through this same Spirit.[130]

Since the Spirit indwells the believer, "we are under obligation" to serve the One to whom we have given our allegiance (8:12; recall 6:12–18). Paul's "you must die" and "you will live" statements contrast God's condemnation and His justification through faith, not physical death versus physical life. While God's Spirit gives life to our souls, there are expectations of us as well: we must put to death the deeds of the body (8:13), referred elsewhere as "deeds of the flesh" (Gal. 5:19–21). What this means is: we are responsible for removing the stumbling blocks that interfere with our walk with God in Christ (Mat. 5:29–30). Wicked habits, vices, addictions, and "every form of evil" (1 Thess. 5:22) must be identified, confronted, and removed. We cannot allow evil behavior to coexist with righteousness. "Men ever think that they are really living when they give way to the flesh whereas in reality they are heading straight for eternal death."[131]

Those who are led by the Holy Spirit are called "sons of God" (8:14), which anticipates an inheritance with Him (Gal. 4:7).[132] Paul builds upon this relationship for a moment to drive home two points: first, its unnaturalness (since we are not natural sons); second, its supreme benefits (since now we are of God's family).¹³³ Jesus is the "only begotten [Son] from the Father" (John 1:14); those who enter into covenant with God *through* His Son are "adopted" sons (8:15). The transaction by which we *become* "sons" is legal and binding, making us fully eligible for an inheritance.¹³⁴ "Abba" is an Aramaic word that indicates a (young) son's affectionate appeal to his father; the Jews of Paul's day used this word as a sacred appeal to God the Father.

The Spirit testifies *with* our spirit—not apart from it—that we are indeed "children of God" (8:16; see Eph. 5:1, 8). The Spirit does this based upon what we have done: He confirms that we have been obedient to the gospel commands by which we are *made* "sons" (including but not limited to baptism—see Gal. 3:26–27). Put another way: He is a legal witness to the reality and legitimacy of our sonship to God. *We* know what we have done, but (Paul says) so does God's *Spirit*. This is supremely important, since our future inheritance—eternal life with God—depends upon the genuineness of our sonship (8:17; see Eph. 1:13–14, 1 Peter 1:3–5).

Christ, as the only begotten of God, is the "heir of all things" (Heb. 1:2). However, He is willing to share this inheritance with those who believe in Him. In this way, we are "heirs *of* God and fellow heirs *with* Christ" (8:17, emphases mine). The promise of this inheritance remains conditioned upon our continued allegiance to Christ. A necessary part of this allegiance is our willingness to "suffer with Him," since we have been called for this very purpose (1 Peter 2:18–21; see 2 Tim. 1:8–12). This suffering refers to whatever trials, losses, or persecutions we face specifically for the sake of Christ and His righteousness (Mat. 5:10–12). It is *not* about suffering the same things the ungodly also face (e.g., broken bones, aging, cancer, etc.). If one will not suffer for Christ, then neither will Christ glorify him.

The Consolation of Hope and Divine Assurance (8:18–39)

Justification by faith provides many spiritual blessings for the believer, but there are also losses and difficult expectations as well. Having just connected the Christian's suffering with future glorification with Christ (recall 8:17), Paul now takes a moment to expound upon this. In some ways, this exposition creates new questions even as it answers others. One thing is for certain: "the sufferings of this present time are not worthy to be compared with the glory that is to be revealed to us" (8:18). In other words, whatever losses we incur in this life for the sake of Christ will be more than compensated in the life to come.

Consequence of the Curse (8:19–22): The word "creation" (8:19) can also be "creature," depending on the context.[135] Here, "creation" seems the most natural conclusion; to translate it "creature" may put a different slant on the entire passage. Even so, there is disagreement over what "creation" involves or does not involve. It appears, by the context and what we know elsewhere in Scripture, this:[136]

- cannot refer to (good) angels, since they have—to our knowledge—never been "subjected to futility" (8:20).[137] "Futility" here means emptiness, vain things, fruitlessness, or whatever does not lead a person to God.[138]
- cannot refer to wicked demons or Satan, for they will never be freed from futility.
- cannot refer only to one who remains an unbeliever, for the same reason as above.
- is not referring only to Christians since Paul mentions them later (8:23–25).

Thus, "creation" refers to the whole of physical nature in general (animals, birds, fish, plants, etc., and the entire inanimate physical world), which includes all men, regardless of their moral standing with God.

Paul's point: since all of creation was originally in subjection to Adam (Gen. 1:28–30), his sin affected everything under him.[139] The entire creation, then, suffers under the curse for his moral disobedience. But there remains an "anxious longing" within creation for the restoration of that which was lost (8:19). This is not meant in a literal sense (as in a rehabilitated planet), but in the grand scheme of God's relationship with humankind. God did not create people (or their world) to suffer, but to live in fellowship with Him. Human suffering is the consequence of human sin; through Christ's redemption this suffering will not last forever. As a result, God's purpose for the "creation"—people and their world—will be fulfilled when the redeemed are brought into God's glory.[140]

This explanation seems unsatisfying to some, since it does not address how the physical creation will be "set free" if it will disappear (8:21). But Paul's language here is figurative—the personification of "the creation" indicates this—not literal; he speaks with a big-picture, end-of-all-things (a.k.a. eschatological) perspective, not about particular details. The physical world suffers for now but not forever; likewise, Christians suffer for now but not forever.

God's curse upon Adam's world was a direct response to Adam's sin (8:20). "Futility" implies hopelessness: without the redemption of human souls, all creation would be pointless. Yet "God's creation is not a grand failure"[141] since the salvation of the part (i.e., the redeemed) satisfies the purpose of the whole (i.e., the physical creation). Put another way: the redeemed could not have *become* "the redeemed" without the context of the entire creation. The "hope" of God's creation is entirely bound up in the redemption of God's people; apart from this salvation, all hope is gone.

Until the realization of this redemption, however, the physical world continues to suffer (8:21). The childbirth analogy (8:22) indicates that something good will come from this suffering, even though the suffering itself may seem unbearable. Likewise, Christians also suffer (8:23)—and Paul did particularly (see Acts 9:15–16, 2 Cor. 11:23–28, 2 Cor. 12:7–10, etc.)—but good will come from this. The "we" reference here seems to refer immediately to Paul's generation—i.e., those who enjoyed the "first fruits of the Spirit"[142]—but includes all Christians, since all endure trials for their faith in Christ.

The Spirit's Intercession (8:23–27): The work of the Spirit within Christians is a pledge of good things to come (2 Cor. 1:21–22): their "adoption as sons"; the "redemption of our body" (recall 8:11); and salvation itself (8:23–24). "In hope we have been saved," because our salvation is in the form of a promise, not yet fully realized or "seen." We have not yet seen God; we remain tethered to this life; we still live under the same curse that God imposed upon the entire world. Our hope is real but pertains to the invisible future, not the visible present (8:25; see 2 Cor. 4:16–18 and Heb. 10:35–36).[143]

The entire creation groans, the Christian groans, and "in the same way the Spirit…intercedes for us with groanings too deep for words" (8:26). "Weakness" (here) refers to our inability to express ourselves adequately to the Father, as regards what is best, what is right, and what agrees with His will; thus, the need for the Spirit's intercession. The Spirit does not groan as we do, as one subjected to the sufferings of this world, but pleads on our behalf.[144] The Spirit "helps our weaknesses"—"helps" comes from a Greek word used only here and in Luke 10:40, where Martha asked Jesus to tell Mary to give her a hand. This is what the word means: to lend or give a helping hand, even though the Spirit does far more than the expression implies.[145]

Paul's expression, "the mind of the Spirit" (8:27), seems to be speaking of the actual mind of God's Spirit—an intelligent Personage of the Godhead distinct from but intimately united with the Father. In any case, God searches the mind of His Spirit, who Himself searches the minds (hearts) of His people. Thus, God the Spirit intercedes for the prayers of the saints, always according to the Father's will.

The Predestination of God's Church (8:28–30): "And we know …" (8:28)—this knowledge is based upon what has already been recorded (Rom. 15:4). The phrase "God causes" is not in the original text but is necessarily implied: men are incapable of causing "all things to work together for good"; only God has repeatedly proven His ability to do this, even against impossible odds. The ultimate outcome—for God, His children, and all of Creation—will be "good," despite the present troubles of this life. "Those who love the Lord," "those who are called,"[146] and "those whom He foreknew" (8:29) all refer to the same people: the redeemed who are in the body of Christ, Christ's spiritual church. The actions described in 8:29–30 are apply to the entire body of believers:[147]

- God **foreknew** the church: He knew prior to its establishment that it would be the only body of the redeemed ("there is one body"—Eph. 4:4).
- God **predestined** the church—the entire body of Christ, not each individual member—to conform to the image of His Son (Eph. 4:11–13). Even so, this idea will be *extended* to each member who "[walks] in the same manner in which [Christ] walked" (1 John 2:6). "This [latter] image, indistinct in the new convert, becomes progressively clearer and distinct as that believer grows in the Christian life."[148] Before Christ's church ever came to be, God foreknew the nature and outcome of it.
- God, having foreknown and predestined this group of believers, then **called** that group out of the world (2 Cor. 6:16–18). No one can come to God who has not been called (invited); no one is called except through His Son (John 14:6) and His Spirit (2 Thess. 2:13–14).

- God then **justified** all those who became part of this called-out group. As with Abraham (recall 4:3), believers are justified by faith and not works of law, and God is the One who credits this justification. In this case, it can be said that the entire group is "justified" since it is made up only of justified people.
- Being foreknown, predestined, called, and justified, the church is **glorified**. Notice this action is in the past tense. The spiritual body of believers is already glorified as Christ's "body" and has received God's Spirit as a pledge (or earnest) (2 Cor. 1:21–22, Eph. 1:13–14). This speaks to reality of the believer's justification and at the same time anticipates a glorious future (as in Eph. 2:6).

Our Victory through God's Justification (8:31–39): "What then shall we say to these things?" (8:31). The temporary sufferings of the world are swallowed up in the manifold blessings of God. He has not withheld anything from His church: if He has given us His Son, He will give us whatever else we need as well (8:32). Since God has justified us, no accusation or charge against Christians will have any legal or binding effect (8:33). Satan's accusations against us are silenced upon Jesus having removed our sins by His blood (Eph. 1:7). Christ has died for us, but He now lives for us and serves as our Intercessor to the Father (8:34).[149] Faithful Christians have nothing short of the highest and most powerful authority *in the universe* supporting, protecting, and advocating for them.

If we are in fellowship with God, then no power can sever us from His salvation (8:35–39). Paul specifically says that it is "the love of Christ" from which we cannot be separated, but in the context, this love is for those who belong to Him. We cannot imagine Paul saying these things to anyone who is not a faithful Christian! Even so, this does not remove or make us immune to trials, heartache, persecution, or even martyrdom; Paul's citation (8:36) from Psalm 44:22 indicates that the Christian's suffering is not a new phenomenon. Nonetheless, these things cannot sever us from God's love for His people (8:37–39). "In the world you have tribulation," Jesus said, "but take courage; I have overcome the world" (John 16:33). Not only are we victorious in Him in our world, but we will also share in the glory of all-powerful and benevolent King (Rev. 3:20–21) in *His* world.[150] We are not only released from our spiritual prison, but we are promised gifts of heaven as well (Eph. 4:7–10).

A Recap of Romans 1—8:

- God's righteousness to humankind is clear in the gospel of Christ (1:16–17). Even though people have been (and continue to be) unrighteous toward *Him*, God continues to show kindness, patience, and love toward *them*. The grace He provides to those who live by faith in Him epitomizes this righteousness.
- "The righteous man shall live by faith": people are incapable of successfully participating in any other system of justification. They have failed to be law-keepers; they cannot redeem themselves through self-righteousness. The gospel of Christ outlines the standard for (or definition of) this "faith" (1:16–17).
- Upon rejecting God's laws and divine influence, people inevitably descend into idolatry, immorality, and depravity (1:18–32). This is as evident in our present generation as it was in all ancient history. Those who profess to be wise today (apart from Christ) are the very ones who promote all sorts of perverse philosophies, deviant lifestyles, and ungodly behavior.
- The purpose of God's kindness is to bring people to their senses so they will demonstrate faith in Him and repent of their sins. A person's conscience intuitively understands godly morality and is expected to respond to this; regardless, every person will be judged according to whatever law under which he lived (2:1–16).
- The Jews, who had much greater advantage than all other people (since they enjoyed a special covenant relationship with God and received His codified law), nonetheless failed to be perfect law-keepers and thus fell under condemnation (2:17–24).
- Neither covenant status nor symbols of that status (such as circumcision) can equal or replace the requirement that God expects of all men: genuine faith in Him (2:25–29).
- All the world stands guilty before God and falls short of His glory—yet Christ has offered Himself as a worthy offering of atonement for all people. This sacrifice (or propitiation) satisfies the divine justice due those under condemnation and provides grace and salvation instead (3:1–31).
- This system of justification by faith has scriptural and historical precedent. We see it manifested particularly through the example of Abraham, whose righteousness by faith was credited to him prior to circumcision and the Law of Moses (4:1–25).

- ❏ Having been justified by faith, the believer "in Christ" enjoys manifold blessings, which include:
  - Peace with God made possible by the "free gift" (grace) of Christ (5:1–21).
  - Newness of life, having died *to* his former allegiance to sin and *with* Christ. He now lives in righteousness to a new Master, which he demonstrates through visible acts of service (6:1–23).
  - Deliverance from the condemnation incurred by his violation of "law" (God's standard of righteousness). Having been freed from this condemnation through Christ's blood, the believer is now able to produce "good fruit" for God (7:1–25) despite continuing to war against sinful temptations.
  - Guidance of the Spirit, since a born-again believer no longer walks according to the "flesh" (his self-serving carnal nature) but enjoys the Spirit's indwelling. His adoption into the family of God entitles him to an inheritance *with* God if he continues to walk by the Spirit (8:1–17).
  - Consolation of the Spirit and divine assurance of a future with God, despite whatever trials or sufferings he endures in this life (8:18–30). God has called the believer into His fellowship, which is secured by his having become part of Christ's church, which is predestined for glory. Having been justified by God, he does not have to worry whether he is justified (or condemned) by anyone else. Because of this, it does not matter what external trials he must face: his soul rests in God's hands (8:31–39).

SECTION THREE: THE RIGHTEOUSNESS OF GOD (9:1—11:36)

HAVING LAID OUT THE DOCTRINE OF JUSTIFICATION, Paul now turns to a different but related subject: the nation of Israel itself. The purpose for this is two-fold. **First,** to show that God was not negligent about promises He had made long ago to Israel. Rather than the gospel being an abandonment of those promises, Paul argues that the gospel of Christ expresses the "righteousness of God" to Israel. **Second,** even though Jews and Gentiles are equal in Christ, the Gentiles owed a tremendous debt of gratitude to the faithful remnant of Jews who had kept the promises of God alive until the gospel's unveiling. This point did not need to be made for long: after the destruction of Jerusalem (in AD 70), ethnic distinctions in the church would become irrelevant. But Paul wanted to set the record straight regarding what had transpired between God and Israel, and where everyone stands who is presently in Christ. The next several chapters (9—11) address all these thoughts.

God Has Not Failed in His Promises to Israel (9:1–33)

Paul begins this discussion by first expressing his great sorrow for—and great disappointment in—the Jewish nation. Only a relatively small number of Jews had come to Christ, even though they were the first to be invited (9:1–5).[151] Paul's disappointment is understandable; yet his compassion, while admirable, is difficult to comprehend, given how often the Jews had maligned, harassed, and even tried to kill him. Nonetheless, Paul cares deeply for his countrymen, and yet is about to say some things that the Jewish mind will find very difficult to hear—and he wants *them* to know that *he* knows this.

The Great Privilege Given to Israel (9:3–5): First, Paul emphatically defends his sincerity by saying, in essence, "The Holy Spirit will confirm that I am not lying." Then, in a shocking admission, Paul states that he would rather be accursed [Greek, *anathema*] if such a sacrifice could secure the salvation of his countrymen (9:3).[152] This does not mean that he would gladly lose his *soul*—and willingly become God's enemy—if it meant the salvation of the Israelite nation, but it does mean that he would gladly give up his *life* for them.[153]

Next, Paul expresses his respect for the Jewish nation and its privileges (9:4–5):

- They are Israelites, direct descendants of the patriarchs Abraham, Isaac, and Jacob, men who were chosen by God to carry out His will on earth.
- They were adopted as God's own people, separated from the rest of the world to serve as a godly example to it.
- They received "the glory"—that is, the holy Presence of God [a.k.a. *shekinah*] as manifested through the cloud which led Israel out of Egypt,

filled the tabernacle, and rested over the ark of the covenant (Exod. 13:31, 40:34–38, and Lev. 16:2).
- They received promises and agreements from God (in His covenant) which were given for their own well-being, which (if honored) would ensure their success (Deut. 28:1–14).
- They were given the Law of Moses, which no other nation received (Psalm 147:19–20).
- They were entrusted with the responsibility to build the original Mosaic tabernacle, and the subsequent Solomonic temple, and ministering to God through it; no other nation had divine permission to build a temple for Jehovah.
- They had the promises of God embedded in the Law and the Prophets concerning their Redeemer (Messiah) and their ultimate regeneration.
- They had the "fathers"—a rich ancestry of righteous men who filled their history, taught them of God, and served as powerful examples of moral integrity. These included the patriarchs, the righteous judges who delivered Israel from their enemies, the righteous kings, the prophets, and the psalmists.
- They were the stock from which the Messiah came. God chose to bring His Son into the world—bringing blessing and salvation to "all the families of the earth" (Gen. 12:3)—through Israel, an honor of the highest magnitude. Notice here (9:5) that Christ is called God "who is over all," which is elsewhere proved in Scripture (John 1:1–2, Titus 2:13).

God's Choice of Israel (9:6–18): "But it is not as though the word of God has failed" (9:6). This picks up where Paul left off in 3:3–6. God had not failed to keep His promises, and God's word had not failed the Jews. Besides, the spiritual people of "Israel" (i.e., Christians) include those who are not Israelites by blood but are those justified by faith (Gal. 3:7–9, 6:15–16). Furthermore, Israel was not the only nation descended from Abraham. The fact that Israel was the only nation of promise was not an accomplishment of Israel but God (9:6–13). Both Esau and Jacob were born to Isaac, but God directed the promise to continue through the lineage of Jacob rather than Esau.[154] God made this designation even before the children were born, so as not to leave the decision to mere men (Gen. 25:23). Likewise, His decision was made before either man had done anything "good or bad," so as not to base the decision upon either man's successes or failures.

"Jacob I loved, but Esau I hated" (9:13, cited from Mal. 1:2) does not mean that Esau was predestined to fail against his own will. It certainly does not have anything to do with the final disposition of Esau's soul: all of Paul's references to Esau *and* Jacob have to do with their earthly circumstances, not their eternal destinations.[155] Rather, Paul says that Esau's self-determined character consistently went against God's divine nature (Gen. 26:34–35, Heb. 12:15–17), and God knew ahead of time that this would be the case.[156] Because of this, He prevented Esau—through His own intervention, and by relying on Esau's self-sabotaging decisions—from receiving the first-born inheritance from Isaac.

Paul's point here (9:14–15) is rhetoric: Did God wrong Esau in choosing Jacob over him? Or did God wrong the nation of Israel in choosing them over all other nations (see Deut. 7:7–8)? Israel had no problem in being God's select people; but just as God's sovereign will selected them (and not others), so He can select others (as well as them). This does not nullify the promises made to Israel, but simply makes promises to others as well. Put another way: the mercy that God showed to Israel was based on divine prerogative; He can show this same prerogative toward (the benefit of) others as well (Exod. 33:19). God did not need to seek Israel's permission or approval in showing mercy to those who are not Israelites. "There is no injustice with God"—i.e., He is just in all His dealings. At the same time, "Mercy is not to be extorted from God by the will of man or the performance of man. This whole exhibition of God's grace, from early times to now, is the result of God's free and sovereign will."[157]

Upon first reading of 9:17, it may appear that God hardens a person's heart independent of his will. Yet Pharaoh—the ruler of Egypt during the time of Israel's exodus (Exod. 5:1ff)—made his own heart hard (or unyielding, resisting; see Heb. 3:7–19) to God *and* Moses.[158] God simply used that condition—and even gave Pharaoh the opportunity to further its progress—for the purpose of glorifying Himself through him. God never hardens anyone's heart that has not already chosen to stubbornly resist His will and refuse the truth. We have previously seen how God "gave over" to depraved minds those who had already abandoned Him and refused to honor Him as God (recall 1:21–27). Likewise, God's "hardening" of one's heart is not something He imposes upon a person but is a consequence of that person's own decisions. The phrase "whom He desires" (9:18) refers, then, to God's divine intervention in the matter: God did not have to show such mercy to Israel, nor did He have to push Pharaoh to the limit that He did. He intervened in both instances for the purpose of furthering His will, which was to bring salvation to all humankind.

Israel's Resistance of God's Will (9:19–33): Paul then anticipates the reply of an obstinate Jew: "Yes, but why does God still find fault in me, since I cannot resist the will of a sovereign God?" (paraphrase of 9:19). The implication is: How can God find fault with Pharaoh, if indeed it was through him that He was glorified? Likewise, how can God find fault with the Jews for murdering His Son, when this is what He needed them to do? If Israel was faithful, God never would have needed to usher in a redeeming Messiah—and the rest of humanity would have suffered as a result! If the Jews had not crucified Jesus, then the world would never have benefited from His sacrificial death! So how can God find fault with those who, despite their own errors, have carried out His divine will?

Such talk is contemptuous since it portrays God's holy will as though it were in league with human rebellion. For this reason, Paul responds forcefully: "On the contrary, who are you, O man, who answers back to God [or, who calls God's judgment into question—MY WORDS]?" (9:20) God does not make people guilty, nor does He punish the innocent; He does not force a person to be saved or condemned. But He does exercise sovereign will upon whomever He chooses. For this reason, He capitalized upon Abraham's already good heart, but hardened Pharaoh's already wicked heart. Likewise, He promised destruction upon the wicked among Israel, but protected Israel's faithful remnant—thereby causing "all things to work together for good [for] those who love God" (Rom. 8:28). Israel had no basis by which to accuse God, just as the clay has no right to judge the potter (9:21; see Isa. 29:16, 45:9, Jer. 18:1–14, and 2 Tim. 2:20–21). Just because God showed kindness to Israel did not mean He had no concern for non-Israelites who were facing "destruction" because of their sinful behavior (9:22).

The OT prophecies foretold of God's offer of salvation to Gentiles (9:25–26; see Isa. 49:5–6, where "nations" are Gentiles). The Jews should have been anticipating this, not scorning it, or standing in the way of it. The quotes from Hosea 1:10 and 2:23 initially applied to the estranged nation of Israel, but—like the dual-fulfillment of many OT prophecies—was finally extended to the Gentiles as well.[159] God's concern was not limited to Israel, but He wanted all people to have fellowship with Him. In quoting from Isa. 10:22–23, Paul makes the point that, despite Israel having a covenant relationship with God (when the Gentiles did not), only a "remnant" (a small proportion) of Israel was "saved" (9:27–28). While Israel had every advantage (recall 9:4–5), this did not guarantee their collective success. The prophets' writings cite numerous instances of their rebellion against God. And, if not for God's merciful intervention, Israel would have become like Sodom and Gomorrah (9:29, citing Isa. 1:9). Thus, Paul counters the Jews' argument by saying, in essence, "Here you [Jews] are upset that God has shown kindness to Gentiles. Yet look how poorly your own nation has responded to the kindness He has shown to you! This not only undermines the strength of your argument but defeats it altogether."

Finally, Paul draws some powerful conclusions (9:30–32). Gentiles who lived faithfully to God were able to obtain righteousness even though they did not have the Law of Moses; the Jews did have the Law, but vainly tried to obtain righteousness through commandment-keeping rather than by faith. God accepts the humble faith of the Gentile but rejects the proud self-righteousness of the circumcised Jew (recall 2:25–29). While God will credit any person with righteousness who has faith in Him, Israel did not exercise such faith, even though they had such good news preached to them (Heb. 4:2).

The Law was meant to lead Israel to Christ, and yet while the Jews had Christ in their very midst, performing numerous and unprecedented miracles, they rejected Him as their Messiah (9:33). Instead of embracing God's Son as their Redeemer, they hardened their heart against Him (Mark 3:5), just as they had long hardened their heart against God (Acts 7:51–53). Thus, the One who was the cornerstone of God's spiritual temple became to many of the Jews a "stumbling block"—something they tripped over because of their blindness (John 9:39–41) and obstinacy (Rom. 10:21; see also 2 Cor. 3:12–16, 1 Peter 2:7–8). Yet, to many Gentiles, this same "stone" became the source of salvation.

God's Righteousness Shown to Israel (10:1–21)

The Jews Sought Justification through Law (10:1–4): Once again, Paul expresses his earnest desire for the salvation of his countrymen, but he also realizes that this will never happen unless they come to Christ. No one could fault the Jews for lacking in religious passion and enthusiasm; in many historical cases, Jews gave up their lives rather than sin against their Law. Yet passion is no replacement for righteousness (10:1-4).[160] Zeal without knowledge leads to erroneous conclusions, not righteous obedience (see John 16:1-3); "Zeal when bigoted and blind is a fearful enemy of change."[161] "Knowledge" here refers specifically to what God revealed in the OT prophecies concerning the Jews' Messiah, as well as the gospel that had been revealed to Paul.

As a rule, the Jews sought justification through law-keeping rather than submission to "the righteousness of God" (10:3)—i.e., that which the gospel declares is true (Rom. 1:17; see Phil. 3:9). The Law of Moses finds its fulfillment in Christ; He is its "end" [lit., aim, goal, or completion]. Thus, the unconverted Jews tried to maintain two incompatible positions: they claimed allegiance to God's Law even while they denied the objective of that Law. As Jesus said (John 5:39-40, 45-47):

> You search the Scriptures because you think that in them you have eternal life; it is these that testify about Me; and you are unwilling to come to Me so that you may have life. … Do not think that I will accuse you before the Father; the one who accuses you is Moses, in whom you have set your hope. For if you believed Moses, you would believe Me, for he wrote about Me. But if you do not believe his writings, how will you believe My words?

Belief in and Confession of Christ (10:5-13): The Jews virtually idolized Moses (John 9:28-29) yet did not fully listen to him. Moses had already stated what Paul has just declared (10:5): to be justified by law, one must keep that law perfectly (see Gal. 5:3 and James 2:10). Yet such justification is impossible, since all people fail to be law-keepers (recall 3:23). However, God has provided through Christ a means for all people to be justified by faith, not law. One does not have to wonder how he will "ascend" or "descend" where it is humanly impossible to go for this justification; he only needs to believe in the One who *has* gone there.[162] "In your heart" (10:6) means "through faith": just as Israel had to demonstrate faith in God in order to find favor with Him, so one must now demonstrate faith in the Son of God for the same reason. Christ has brought the message of salvation down from heaven; but He has also descended into—and *returned* from—the grave itself to make it real and viable (10:6-7; see Eph. 4:7-10).

We are to understand "confessing" and "believing" here (10:8-10) in the context of Paul's discussion. The substance of one's confession is that "Jesus is Lord"—that is, that He indeed came down from heaven, having been sent by God (John 6:32-33, 1 John 2:22-23). Likewise, the substance of one's belief must be that God did indeed raise Jesus from the grave, for without this there is no hope for overcoming the curse of sin (recall 8:20-22; see 1 Cor. 15:13-19). By believing that God resurrected His Son, one also believes that God will raise *himself* from the death of his spiritual condemnation.

One's confession of Jesus' divine nature and belief in His divine power over death constitutes the basis of his faith in God—a faith which has been defined by the gospel of Christ. "Confessing" and "believing" are not the only actions required for salvation but are *at least* required. Paul is not saying, "Just say 'Jesus is Lord' and acknowledge His resurrection, and there is nothing else you must do to be saved." Instead, to "confess" means to speak and live in agreement with that confession; to "believe" means to do whatever else is necessary to support such convictions. In fact, it is possible to believe without confessing (John 12:42-43), just as it is possible to confess without believing (Luke 6:46). In such cases, justification by faith is impossible because genuine faith has not yet been demonstrated.

No one who confesses and believes in Christ will "be disappointed" [lit., put to shame; having cause for regret] (10:11-13).[163] This is true for at least the three reasons Paul has put forward in the context:

- ❏ Christ has made salvation possible and available for every person who comes to Him in faith—i.e., who comes to Him confessing and believing (Acts 2:21, 4:12, 15:7-11).
- ❏ Christ has given sufficient proofs that He is of heaven and that He did resurrect from the dead (John 10:37-38, Acts 1:3).
- ❏ Christ promises salvation to every person who obeys Him—the necessary implication of confessing and believing. No one who does what He requires will seek Him in vain.

Salvation is not—and never has been—predicated entirely upon human works. Yet salvation is impossible without human faith, and "faith without works is dead" (James 2:26). Salvation is a gift of God, not something we could have acquired on our own (Titus 3:4-7). The Jews often missed this point for themselves, then tried to impose their own wrongful thinking upon Gentile proselytes (see Acts 15:7-11). "Instead of compelling a Greek

[Gentile] to become like a legalistic Jew, this legalistic Jew must drop his legalism and become like a believing Greek."[164]

No Excuse for Failing to Believe in Christ (10:14–21): For one to hear this good news of God's salvation, someone must preach it (10:14–15). ("Preacher" here does not refer to a full-time position, as we are familiar with today, but simply means a herald or proclaimer, which could be any believer.[165]) Paul here alludes to the OT prophets who preached and proclaimed the promises of God—all of which were fulfilled in Christ. Such men were "sent," which means they did not speak on their own authority but heaven's. Having such a heavenly proclamation, they were worthy of commendation ("How beautiful are the feet of those who bring good news"—quoted from Isa. 52:7). Paul's point: the Jewish prophets long anticipated the message of Christ's gospel. Thus, if anyone should have responded favorably to this gospel, it should have been the Jews themselves.

Yet Israel also had a long history of choosing not to obey good news (10:16).[166] The prophet Isaiah asked in exasperation of this failure to respond, "Lord, who has believed our report?" (Isa. 53:1). In addressing this more forcefully, Paul first states the obvious: "faith [in Christ] comes from hearing, and hearing by the word of Christ" (10:17). It is a matter of fact that Jews could not confess or believe in Christ if they had never heard of Him (i.e., in prophecy). Thus, Paul rhetorically poses the question, in essence: "Maybe they have never heard of Him?"[167] Yet for centuries the Jews had heard the prophets' "voice" (10:18; quote is from Psalm 19:4).

Paul continues rhetorically: "Maybe the Jews just didn't understand?" Yet even as far back as Moses, God had been prophesying of a universal salvation (10:19; quote is from Deut. 32:21); and Isaiah prophesied that the Gentiles ("nation") would be recipients of this salvation (10:20; quote is from Isa. 65:1). Paul concludes his point (10:21): the problem was not that the Jews had not heard or could not understand the gospel of Christ; instead, it was that their hearts were "disobedient" and "obstinate" toward God's prophets to begin with (see Isa. 65:2, Jer. 6:16–19, Amos 4:6–12, and Acts 7:51–53). Thus, the Gentiles "found" God, even though they had long been ignorant of Him; in contrast, the Jews resisted the Son of God, even though they were blessed with divine oracles concerning Him (recall 3:1–2, 9:3–5).[168]

In a modern application, it is nearly impossible that anyone in the world today could claim that they "never have heard" of the word of Christ (10:18).

Bibles are everywhere and easy to obtain; because of the Internet, God's word more accessible than ever before in all human history. Even though the gospel of Christ is not always proclaimed completely or accurately, there is enough awareness of it—and the resources to better study it—to adequately inform every person of his moral responsibility to God. What God has done through His Son has been proclaimed everywhere, so that the world is without excuse for remaining ignorant of Him (Acts 17:30–31).

God's Righteousness Shown to Gentiles (11:1–36)

God's Gracious Choice of Israel (11:1–6): Even though the nation of Israel had long been "disobedient and obstinate"—and even though God punished them for this resistance—it is not accurate to say that God had rejected His people *because* He punished them. The fact that His Son was born an Israelite is proof of this. Paul made this even more personal: the fact that he himself (a Jew) was a citizen of the kingdom was also proof of this (11:1)—and no one was prouder of his ancestral heritage than Paul (2 Cor. 11:22, Gal. 1:13–14). "God has not rejected His people" (11:2)—while a strong and definitive statement, it does not mean that God justified all Jews simply because they were Jews. God justifies no person apart from his faith, and faith requires demonstration (obedience to God's laws), not ethnic status. No Israelite could be pleasing to God who did not demonstrate faith in Him (John 8:24, 8:37–45, Acts 13:46, Heb. 11:6, etc.).

On the other hand, even during Israel's darkest hours, there had always remained a remnant of believers who held fast to God's promises and obeyed His commandments. The prophet Elijah once claimed that "I alone am left" as a faithful Israelite, yet God revealed, "I have kept for Myself seven thousand men who have not bowed the knee to Baal" (11:2–4; see 1 Kings 19:13–18). While many Israelites had succumbed to apostasy, a faithful remnant was sufficient to warrant God's continued providence toward that nation. The promises remained alive through the steadfast faith of those believers. However, the fact that God entrusted Israel with these promises was not Israel's choice, but His (11:5–6). This grace—a gift of God— removed any basis for Israel's boasting, for God could have just as easily chosen any other nation for this same purpose. This remnant's preservation was not dependent upon their "works" (of Law) but their faith in God.

God's Salvation Given to Gentiles (11:7–15): "What then?" Paul asks rhetorically (11:7). In other words, "What is the natural conclusion to the matter under discussion?" It is this: Israel failed (as a whole) to be justified through zeal and human effort. "[T]hose who were chosen obtained" justification—the "chosen" here are those Israelites (and others) who sought God through faith and not self-righteousness.[169] "[A]nd the rest were hardened"—referring to Israelites who sought God through any means other than faith. "Hardened" means to close one's heart to the kindness of God and opportunity for divine salvation (recall 2:4). It is a process which these people began by having turned away from God but which God completed, blinding their eyes to the truth which they had so systematically rejected (see 2 Thess. 2:10–12). To underscore his point, Paul cites examples from the OT (11:8–10; quotes are from Isa. 6:9–10 and Psalm 69:22–23).

While not all of Israel "stumbled," the many who did stumble gave opportunity for God to show His kindness to others (11:11). Thus, "salvation has come to the Gentiles," which was God's eternal purpose all along. Ideally, having offered to the Gentiles that which was promised to Israel would "make jealous" those Israelites who still resisted Christ's gospel (recall 10:19–20). The intent was for them to draw near to God by faith; proportionately few, however, responded in this way (see Acts 13:44–49). Yet if God's goodness is sustained despite the Jews' rejection of Christ's gospel, then how much good will He bring to those who accept it!

Paul then addresses the Gentile Christians directly (11:12–16). He wants them to know that he is not saying such things to alienate his countrymen, but to provoke them to seek God through faith. To bring Jews to the gospel through his ministry to the Gentiles would "magnify" Paul's ministry: it would make it even more worthwhile. If by having rejected their Messiah the Jews were instrumental in ushering in salvation to the world, then their acceptance of Christ would lead to "life from the dead"—a resurrection of the hope of Israel through the power of their Redeemer.

The Remnant Preserves the Whole (11:16–32): The "first piece of dough" and "root" illustrations (11:16) allude to the "first fruits" concept in the Law of Moses (Lev. 23:10, Num. 15:18–21; see 1 Cor. 15:20). If one dedicated a remnant of his crop to God, then God would bless his entire harvest. The lesser portion sanctified the greater; the parts sanctified the whole. The "root" is the faithful remnant of Israel[170] who kept the promises of the Redeemer alive through their faith in God; the "branches" are those Jews and Gentiles who were recipients of these promises through their acceptance of the gospel.

Paul then expounds upon this thought to make an essential point (11:17–24). Using an olive tree analogy, Jews are as "branches" which came naturally from the root. Gentiles are as "wild" branches—unnatural, uncultivated, foreign branches which had to be "grafted" in. The "olive tree" itself is Christ, whose identity and mission as Messiah sprouted directly from the root of God's promises and prophecies to Israel.[171] The message to the Gentiles here is: "do not be arrogant toward the branches" (11:18)—i.e., do not forget that it was not you (Gentiles) but the Jewish remnant who kept the promises of God alive by faith. Do not, therefore, hold Jews in contempt or think lightly of their role in the gospel of Christ. Gentiles did not support the root but were blessed because the root supported them.

Paul then anticipates a Gentile's smug response: "Branches were broken off so that I might be grafted in" (11:19). In other words, "Because not all Jews were faithful, we have a legitimate right to take their places." While Paul agrees with this (11:20), he clarifies the situation. If Jews are justified by faith, then Gentiles are justified in the same way; however, if Jews are removed because of unbelief, then Gentiles will be removed for the same reason. "Do not be conceited, but fear"—i.e., do not be arrogant because of the great privilege you now enjoy. God's kindness is conditional; if the conditions are no longer met, then His kindness will be replaced with divine wrath (11:22).[172] Even so, there is still hope for those Jews who had not yet believed: if they do respond to God in faith, then they who were once "broken off" will also be "grafted in" (11:23–24).

This last section of this chapter (11:25–36), which is also the last section of Paul's thesis on "justification by faith" (1:16—11:36), will be misunderstood if the context is abandoned. Paul admits that a "mystery" has been declared: what once was not fully known has now been revealed by God. A passage parallel to this is Eph. 3:1–11, where "mystery" refers to the inclusion of Gentiles into God's covenant of salvation through His gospel. This once-mysterious revelation could not have been possible except for a "partial hardening" of Israel (11:25)—a hardening which God did not create but used to His advantage.

This begs the question (and has been the source of much debate): what is the difference between a "partial hardening" and a complete hardening? If the entire nation of Israel had been hardened, it could not have been saved at all but would have been cursed and fully destroyed.[173] As it was, the remnant of faithful believers preserved the nation of Israel, to the extent that God's purpose could be carried out through them. Some commentators believe the "fullness of the Gentiles" refers to a particular number of Gentiles to be saved throughout history; once that quota is reached, humanity will be radically changed (or ended).[174] Such interpretations seem unsupported and unnatural. Nowhere else in Scripture is there a reference to a set number of people to be saved.

It seems more natural to read Paul's words as a reference to an era (or period) rather than a specific number of people. In this sense, "the fullness of the Gentiles" refers to the time in which believing Gentiles entered the kingdom of God while unbelieving "sons of the kingdom" (Jews) did not (see Mat. 8:11–12). This era would end upon the destruction of Jerusalem (AD 70), since after that time the Jewish nation lost all distinction as God's covenantal people. The only covenant God now acknowledges is the one made between Him and a believer in Christ. Israel's "partial hardening" continued until that covenant was the only one that existed; afterward, it no longer mattered.

"And so all Israel will be saved" (11:26)—a phrase often misunderstood and misinterpreted. This cannot mean every single Israelite will be saved, for God will not save anyone who refuses to put his faith in Him. "All Israel" is in parallel to how the redemption of the "whole creation" through the salvation of its remnant (recall 8:18–22): the whole will be justified (made worthwhile) by the redemption of the part (recall 9:29). In other words, the nation of Israel would have been a worthless cause (since Israel rejected God for idols, then rejected His Son for a temple) except for the relatively small portion that did not reject Him. Without this remnant, Israel as a nation would have disappeared from the face of the earth, just as many other nations were exterminated because of their sins (cf. Isa. 1:4–9).

As it is, the faithfulness of the remnant justifies God's having given them the promises and favor that He did. Furthermore, these blessings ushered in the Savior of the world, so that all who are saved—whether Jews or Gentiles—owe a debt of gratitude to these believers. The quote (in 11:26–27) is from Isa. 59:20–21 and anticipates a time during the reign of Messiah when the shame of Israel's sins and captivities will be removed upon the establishment of a new covenant (see Jer. 31:31–34 and Heb. 8:8–13). The gospel of God outlines this new covenant, which Christ brought to life with His own blood (Mat. 26:26–29). Those who enter this covenant become members of Christ's church.

The unconverted Jew is an "enemy" to the believing (Gentile) Christian since both people's beliefs are incompatible and antagonistic to each other (11:28). However, this does not mean God has no concern for an unbelieving Jew—or for all unbelieving Israelites. God's gifts and calling are irrevocable (11:29) which means He has not acted kindly toward Israel in vain, nor does He regard every unbelieving Jew as a hopeless cause. Just as He mercifully gave salvation to the Gentiles, though they were once disobedient to Him, God can just as easily do the same for disobedient Jews (11:30–31). God has "shut up all in disobedience" (11:32)—i.e., He has silenced those who failed to justify themselves apart from faith in Him (Gal. 3:22); He has put all (sinners) together into one group, regardless of ethnicity (recall 3:9–12, 23).

God's Righteousness Extolled (11:33–36): These final verses appropriately express Paul's personal appreciation for the work of God toward the salvation of men (quotes are from Isa. 40:13–14). This salvation is not of human design but is "according to His own purpose and grace which was granted us in Christ Jesus from all eternity" (2 Tim. 1:9). Whatever God has done has been for our human benefit and to the praise of His own glory. "For from Him and through Him and to Him are all things"—see also 1 Cor. 8:6, Eph. 4:6, and Col. 1:15–17, where both God the Father and God the Son are similarly praised. This hymn of praise (a.k.a. doxology) also serves as a fitting conclusion to the doctrinal section of *Romans* (chapters 1—11), wherein "the righteousness of God" is revealed through the gospel and every person is justified by his faith in this righteousness: "Amen."

Section Four:
The Righteousness of God Produces a Righteous Life (12:1—15:33)

Having successfully argued the concept of "justification by faith," Paul now proceeds to the practical application of his letter to the Roman Christians. Once a person is justified by faith according to the righteousness of God, that person is expected to exhibit the attitudes and characteristics of one who has been redeemed. His heart and conduct must agree with the God in whom he has put his faith. Having entered a covenant relationship with God, he must now continue to abide by its terms. The information in this section (12:1—15:33) is as relevant to Christians today as it was to those in the first century, as we will see.

Righteous Conduct toward Fellow Christians (12:1–21)

The Believer's Transformation by Grace (12:1–2): One's transformation from a condemned, helpless sinner into a child of God who walks "in newness of life" (Rom. 6:4) must affect every aspect of his life in a full surrender to Christ (12:1–2). "Presenting" oneself to God calls to mind the sacrificial system of the Law of Moses. The ancient Levitical priests presented offerings and sacrifices to God upon His holy altar before the tabernacle. Jesus presented Himself before God as the perfect, once-for-all sacrifice for sinners upon another altar—His cross (Heb. 9:11–14). The Christian also presents himself before God as a spiritual offering. His is not a bloody sacrifice, as is needed for atonement; it is not a dead sacrifice, like the sheep and bulls offered on the ancient altar. Rather, he is a "living and holy sacrifice": he is (ideally) always prepared (i.e., consecrated) for service. The offering of animals was merely a legal conformity to the Law; but a "living sacrifice" implies one's functional life worship. Worship involves three main aspects: service, sacrifice, and reverence; Paul touches on all three in this brief but powerful passage. "Spiritual service" can also be rendered "logical worship"[175]: it is spiritual because of its type; it is intelligent (or rational) because of those who offer it, as opposed to unthinking animals which were laid upon the altar.

This "transformation" must not be the mere cessation of outward worldly behaviors (12:2). It must instead begin from within. "To acceptably worship Him [God] we must offer what pleases Him. Our offerings must honor Him. But we must not only consciously offer to Him things that please Him, we must pleasingly offer them."[176] "Conform" means to imitate the likeness of something; "transform" means to be *changed* from one form to another. Being "conformed to this world" means to identify with it; genuine transformation, however, requires a complete renewing of one's mind (Eph. 4:22–24). One whose heart is "conformed to this world" cannot properly offer gifts and sacrifices to God, being hostile to Him (recall 8:6–9). Those justified by faith must change (i.e., transform) into the image of Him to whom they have entrusted their souls. This change will be visible, radical, and life-altering; "The renewed mind induces a new life."[177] This is in accordance with the will of God, which is always "good and acceptable and perfect." God instructs us in what is acceptable service worship (Heb. 12:28–29).

Every Part Contributes to the Whole (12:3–8): This next section (12:3–8) is like what Paul has said elsewhere (1 Cor. 12:12–28). Even though each Christian fulfills a priestly action in his service to God (1 Peter 2:9), no Christian is to think himself "more highly" than any other. Humility is the grease that keeps the machinery of Christian service effective and efficient (Mat. 18:1–4). The opposite of humility is pride, which only produces friction, tension, and unnecessary breakdowns in fellowship.

The analogy between the church and a human body (12:4–5) is an excellent one. The body is a working unit, comprised of smaller parts, organs, and systems. No part works alone, even though some do have a greater responsibility than others (e.g., the heart versus a finger). All its parts are meant to work in concert, not separately. So it is with the church: the "many members" have different functions, responsibilities, and measures of faith, but no one person acts alone or calls himself "the church" (or even "a" church). Christ's body is not divisible; despite any apparent dissimilarities, we "are all one in Christ Jesus" (Gal. 3:29). Therefore, each person's gifts, service, talents, exhortation, etc., must not be compared to another's, for this serves no good purpose. Christians are never in competition with each other.

God gives these "gifts"—whether miraculous (as was sometimes the case in Paul's day) or not (as in our present case)—to Christians according to God's grace (12:6a). This implies three necessary conclusions. First, we cannot boast in what we have received, since we are not responsible for having created the gift (1 Cor. 1:30–31). Second, God only gives gifts for good reason; thus, it is the Christian's responsibility to discover the purpose of his gifts and to exercise them according to that purpose (12:6b–8). Third, all Christians do not have the same measure of faith (12:3)—that is, not all have the same capacity and/or comprehension to put into ideal practice the gift(s) that God makes available to them. Thus, one who prophesies, serves, teaches, exhorts, gives, leads, or shows mercy is to do so to the best of his ability—which may be different than someone else who exercises the same gift. Regardless of one's type of service, all that Christians do must be to the glory of God and "for the common good" of the body (1 Cor. 12:7).

What God Expects Christians to Do (12:9–21): Having instructed us to exercise our individual gifts, Paul follows with a list of general acts of service. These virtues and behaviors form a composite picture of what every Christian ought to "look" like:

- **"Let love be without hypocrisy"** (12:9)[178]: Love is to be "unfeigned" (1 Peter 1:22–23) and visibly demonstrated (1 John 3:18). Fake love or love without action is useless to the one who claims it, the one to whom it is directed, and the One in whose honor it is offered. "Feigned love is hate disguised."[179]
- **"Abhor what is evil; cling to what is good"** (12:9): The thought is: a Christian cannot merely dislike sin but must hate it; it must repulse him. Likewise, he cannot passively agree with what is good, but must tenaciously pursue and lay hold of it (1 Thess. 5:21–22).
- **"Be devoted to one another in brotherly love"** (12:10): A Christian is to honor the family relationship we all enjoy in Christ (2 Peter 1:7). He must not merely acknowledge the existence of this relationship but devote himself to its growth, success, and propagation.
- **"Give preference to one another in honor"** (12:10): Paradoxically, true greatness (in God's sight) comes through humility, which requires a preferment of others over oneself (Mat. 20:26–28, Phil. 2:3–4). This also implies giving others mercy and the benefit of doubt as opposed to rushing to judgment (Mat. 7:1–2, James 4:11–12).
- **"not lagging behind in diligence, fervent in spirit, serving the Lord"** (12:11): In other words, whatever service we render to the Lord must

be offered with zeal, enthusiasm, and purposeful intention. Laziness and slothfulness are not hallmarks of godly virtue but imply disrespect and unbelief. Cold indifference ruins "gifts" offered to God (Mal. 1:6–14); plastic or irreverent service cannot honor Christ and provides no benefit to His people. Instead, we are to be "fervent [lit., boiling (hot)]" with zeal and earnestness, as should be our love toward one another (1 Peter 1:22.)

- ❏ **"rejoicing in hope, persevering in tribulation"** (12:12): This is similar to what has already been said (recall 5:3–5; see Mat. 5:10–12, James 1:2–4, 1 Peter 1:6–9, etc.). All Christians have need of endurance (Heb. 10:36), but without a sufficient hope, there is no incentive for this. Hope gives life to perseverance; without one, the other dies. A strong and realistic hope contributes to a strong and enduring faith (2 Tim. 1:12).

- ❏ **"devoted to prayer"** (12:12): This does not refer to incidental prayers, but one's commitment to prayer as a lifestyle (Eph. 6:18, Col. 4:2). Prayer is our lifeline from earth to heaven; without it, we cannot access any spiritual blessings "in Christ" (Eph. 1:3) or petition God on behalf of others. Prayer is an act of faith: those who do not pray imply that they do not really believe God will help them. When we pray, we are to put our full belief in the God to whom we pray and "not lose heart" (Luke 18:1, James 1:5–8).

- ❏ **"contributing to the needs of the saints, practicing hospitality"** (12:13): An important aspect of Christian fellowship involves sharing what we have with Christians who are in need (Gal. 6:9–10, James 2:14–17, 1 John 3:17–18), which produces a form of equality among the brethren (2 Cor. 8:12–15). "Hospitality" comes from a Greek root word which means "fond of guests" or "lover of strangers."[180] This refers especially to Christian "strangers" or "prisoners" (Heb. 13:1–3). Hospitality is more than just inviting someone over for dinner; it also is kindness toward and acceptance of those in the church who might have otherwise gone unnoticed.

- ❏ **"Bless those who persecute you"** (12:14): This is just as Jesus instructed us (Mat. 5:44–47, Luke 6:27–28). This does not mean, "Be indifferent toward the harm inflicted upon you," or, "Pretend it doesn't hurt." It means, "Do your part to absorb the loss or harm inflicted upon you so that God may be glorified in your choosing to do what is right despite the consequences."

- ❏ **"Rejoice …, weep …"** (12:15): Just as our possessions are common between us (as needed), so our hearts are to be as one heart (1 Cor.

12:26, James 5:13–20). We should never be so self-absorbed that we think only of our own welfare and neglect the needs and concerns of others. Likewise, we are not to begrudge another's prosperity ("If only that had happened to me!") or gloat over his misfortune ("It's a good thing that didn't happen to me!").

- **"Be of the same mind"** (12:16): This is a recurring theme in Paul's epistles (1 Cor. 1:10, Phil. 1:27, 2:1–5, etc.). When one becomes "wise in [his] own estimation," he makes himself a judge of others' intentions and conduct, using himself as a standard rather than Christ.[181] "Same mind" does not mean "same opinion," unanimous consensus, or groupthink. The context has to do with a shared resolve to honor Christ's doctrine. No group of Christians will ever be of the exact same opinions; however, every church that invokes Christ's name must conform to and habitually practice His teaching (1 John 2:4–6, in principle).
- **"Never pay back evil for evil … be at peace with all men"** (12:17–20): It is natural for the worldly individual to seek vengeance and retaliation for crimes committed against him. To "take revenge" means to "take satisfaction for an injury by inflicting punishment [or judgment] on the offender."[182] Yet Jesus set a different example for us: when treated unjustly, He "kept entrusting Himself to [God] who judges righteously" (1 Peter 2:23) instead of taking justice into His own hands. Christians are to be peacemakers (Mat. 5:9) and pursuers of peace (Heb. 12:14), "so far as it depends upon you." In some (many?) cases, peace will not be possible, but division will result instead. If the word of God divides, so be it (Luke 12:51–53), but it must not be our pride, vengeance, or irresponsibility that causes division. "Coals" are not meant to inflict injury or punishment but force a change of heart in the perpetrator by shaming him with kindness and good deeds (Prov. 25:21–22).
- **"Do not be overcome by evil, but overcome evil with good"** (12:21): Or "Stop being conquered by the evil (thing or man)," but "drown the evil in the good."[183] In sum, "put on the new self" (Col. 3:10) in which Christ reigns, not evil. To "overcome evil with good" is a principle unknown in all ancient heathen literature; modern versions of this (which often confuse it with "pacifism") are only imitations of this. A Christian may not overcome another person's evil directed against him, but he can overcome evil in himself.

Elders should direct to this passage every Christian who comes to them and asks, "What should I be doing?" or "What can I do to help this congregation?" Nearly every Christian can do nearly every one of these actions. Furthermore, these are all *basic expectations*: they are the *least* that should be done.

Righteous Conduct toward Secular Government (13:1–14)

Christians and Secular Authority (13:1-5): The proper response to governmental authority might have been a difficult subject for Christians living in the capital of a pagan, ungodly empire. This remains a difficult subject even today, although some Christians deal with it more emotionally than realistically. In an extreme view, one might assume that allegiance to Christ nullifies any allegiance to his government. On the other extremity, one might assume that Christians are to obey whatever the government says in order not to violate passages like this one (13:1-5).

While God does not prevent governments from being wicked or unjust—even toward Christians—He is concerned with how His saints conduct themselves toward them. This is the main reason for Paul's instructions here. Some related passages include:

- **Acts 5:29:** "We must obey God rather than men"—Christians cannot obey laws of the land that violate our pre-eminent allegiance to God. On the other hand, this passage does not teach that we cannot follow *any* civil laws made by ungodly men. The fact that authority originates with God is why we are to obey such laws, not because of the moral disposition of the ones who make (or enforce) them.
- **Acts 25:11:** Paul admits that if he is guilty of violating civil law, and that law condemns him to execution, then he would freely submit to this. Paul could never have held this view if indeed it violated the gospel of Christ.
- **1 Tim. 2:1–2:** Christians are to pray for those in authority, for their rulers' sakes as well as their own. Notice that the moral disposition of the "kings" is irrelevant. Consider Eccles. 8:2–9 for parallel (but less direct) thoughts.
- **Titus 3:1:** Christians are "to be subject to rulers, to authorities, to be obedient [to their laws], to be ready for every good deed" (bracketed words added). Again, the moral disposition of those in authority is

- irrelevant here. The issue here concerns our respect for God's authority, not necessarily whether we agree with the laws of the land.
- ❏ **1 Peter 2:13–17:** Christians are to honor those who have governing authority over their land, wherever they live. The purpose is clearly stated: "that by doing right you may silence the ignorance of foolish men." By obeying the laws of the land, those who might charge Christians of being lawbreakers, traitors, or anarchists would have no valid accusation.

Paul's (and Peter's) instructions on one's attitude toward government are not meant to be comprehensive but are general and apply to normal circumstances. Unusual, extraordinary, and even unprecedented circumstances require more specific direction than what we have been given, even though Paul's words here still provide a foundation for *all* such discussions. Human laws are, in the most basic sense, meant to govern society, protect the rights and lives of law-abiding citizens, and punish criminals. Such laws are *not* meant to define, or interfere with, what Christians are called to do; even Jesus spoke of the separation of church and state (Mat. 22:17–22). The idea of seeking "permission" from governing authorities to conduct our God-given responsibilities as Christians manifests a great misunderstanding of this passage. On the other hand, becoming a Christian does not free a person from all the constraints of and obligations to civil law. Since God has given permission for secular authorities to exist, to purposely (or carelessly) disobey them defies God's own ordinance (law).

However, just because God allows a government to exist does not mean He sanctions its every decision or legislation. The Roman Empire was anything but godly; Caesar Nero (ruled AD 54–68), the emperor who reigned at the time when Paul wrote *Romans*, descended into monstrosities and madness; yet Rome and Nero served God's purpose until the time when He brought them both to an end. "God may and does tolerate governments in doing wrong, just as he does men in sinning, but he sanctions neither the wrong nor the sin."[184] To "submit" to such a government does not mean we do so blindly or without understanding; rather, it means we put ourselves under the control of this government voluntarily and for the right motives—above all, to honor God and set a good example for men.

Disobedience to human laws not only brings punishment from the government itself, but also a condemnation from God.[185] Unnecessary violation of civil law would then be against our conscience as well as against the governing authority. In this passage (13:3–4), Paul supports capital punishment (i.e., execution by the sword) and expects governments to exercise this right as a "minister of God" in the case of those who deserve it.

Rendering All that Is Due (13:6–10): No Christian likes to pay taxes, especially to a secular government, but this does not (in itself) violate one's allegiance to Christ (13:6–7). It has been argued that paying taxes to a godless government constitutes an endorsement of its godless practices, but these are often separate issues. In paying taxes, Christians are honoring God's authority, not giving an endorsement to all that that government does with its money. For example, Jesus supported paying the Jewish the temple tax (Mat. 17:24–27), even though this indirectly supported those who would later conspire against His life (John 11:49–53). Jesus also supported paying taxes to Rome—the very government which would later authorize His own execution. His principle of "[Rendering] to Caesar the things that are Caesar's; and to God the things that are God's" is still relevant and applicable (Mat. 22:15–22).[186] Paul concurs: "Render to all what is due them"—the one to whom the debt is owed is not the point here; rather, it is that God's people are not to be remiss in paying their debts. Debts are like promises; refusing to pay them is equivalent to breaking a promise. Just as God is faithful to fulfill all His promises to men, so Christians must be faithful to fulfill theirs.

The deepest "debt" any of us has toward one another is not in the form of taxation, but love (13:8–10).[187] Paul uses "debt" here figuratively, as a sort of play on words from the previous discussion on taxation. Love is, in essence, a "debt" that will never be paid up, a duty that is never complete. As God's love for us is continual and unconditional, so should ours be toward others, and especially toward the brethren (Gal. 6:9–10, 1 Peter 1:21, 1 John 4:7–21, etc.). Love is the foundation of all moral laws (Gal. 5:14), since all other laws of God rest upon and find their completion in love.[188] Love is never a replacement for God's law but is in fact a performance of it.[189] The demonstration of love is itself the "royal law" (James 2:8; see Mat. 7:12), since it reflects the King's own nature (1 John 4:8). One who shows love to his neighbor will always do him good and not harm, regardless of what action is taken (cf. Luke 10:29–37).

Now Is the Time to Act (13:11–14): Seeing that we have a finite existence on this earth, we have little time to carry out all our Christian duties and obligations. "[K]nowing the time" [KJV, "it is high time"] indicates a sense of urgency, not complacency or procrastination (13:11). To "awaken from sleep" is a mild rebuke; in other words, "If you have been lethargic in your moral responsibilities, it is time to wake up and get busy!" There is always a need for this admonition; "Few Christians are ever as wide awake as they should be."[190]

While the world sinks into darkness and oblivion, Christians are to be a source of light and activity (see Mat. 5:13–16, Eph. 5:7–14, and 1 Thess. 5:4–11). This means our behavior must match the seriousness of our ministry. "The night is almost gone"—in this context (13:12), "night" refers to this earthly life; "day" refers to an endless life with God. One must "lay aside" the "deeds of darkness"—i.e., the attitudes and behaviors that are associated with the corrupted earthly life (Rom. 8:12–13, Gal. 5:19–21, Col. 3:5–10, etc.). In place of these things, he must "put on" that which God gives him: the "armor of light." "Let us behave properly as in the day" (13:13)—i.e., let us live as though we are already in the eternal "day" of fellowship with God. The following behaviors have no place in that fellowship:

- **Carousing and drunkenness:** "Carousing" comes from a Greek word [*komos*] which implies revelry, rioting, and a "letting loose" of one's inhibitions.[191] It is associated with drinking parties and frolicking in the streets at night, especially in honor of Bacchus, the Greek god of wine and revelry (cf. 1 Peter 4:3). A "kegger," rave, or cocktail party would be a modern equivalent to this.
- **Sexual promiscuity and sensuality:** "Sexual promiscuity" refers to lying down on a couch or bed—in this context, for the purpose of sexual intercourse.[192] "Sensuality" refers to unrestrained lust, filthy-mindedness, or any kind of sexual indulgence (Eph. 4:19). With such easy access to pornography by way of the Internet and movies, this is an especially dangerous behavior for Christians of all ages to avoid today.
- **Strife and jealousy:** These refer to quarreling, bickering, and contention. These behaviors also include the worldly attitudes that spawn them, as in coveting what someone else has or being unhappy that they have it (James 3:13–18).

"But put on the Lord Jesus Christ"—lit., clothe yourself with Christ (Gal. 3:27). In ancient times, a king would put royal raiment (garments) upon a person whom that king wanted to honor and have identified with him (cf. Esther 6:7–8, Zech. 3:3–5, Luke 15:22, etc.; for the opposite idea, see Psalm 109:29). Such honor and identification, of course, required that person to be responsible and rightly represent the one whose clothes he wore (Mat.

22:8–12). The parallel to being clothed with Christ is obvious, except for two differences: first, we do not put on a garment *belonging* to Christ, but we put on *Christ*; second, He does not force us to put Him on but only provides the opportunity. Whether or not we put Him on is up to each one of us.

Righteous Conduct of the Strong and Weak (14:1—15:13)

Paul now turns his attention to another aspect of Christian duty: dealing with those who are "weak in faith." While primary responsibility lies with the "strong," since these know better and are expected to exercise a more mature disposition, both parties are to accept one another in a mutually beneficial arrangement (15:7; see 1 Cor. 8:1–13, 10:14–33, and Col. 2:16–23).

Differences of Conscience (14:1–12): To "accept" a fellow believer (14:1) does not mean here merely to tolerate, as when one endures with gritted teeth someone else's screaming child in a restaurant. It means to receive such a person into fellowship, to treat like family, as the father did his prodigal son in Luke 15:11ff. "Weak" here does not mean incompetent or unwilling, but unable, due to the (yet) lack of mature faith, knowledge, or experience. The strong brother is not to accept a weaker brother only to criticize his motives and actions, but as a fellow and equal brother in Christ (Eph. 3:6, Gal. 3:28).[193]

To illustrate this, Paul uses examples of eating meats versus vegetables, or the honoring of one day (i.e., a religious holy day) versus regarding all days equally. While we can still use these same examples, the principle employed here goes far beyond them. Each believer belongs to God, not to another believer (1 Cor. 6:19–20); each Christian is a servant of Christ and is thus not a slave to another brother's preference or opinion (1 Cor. 7:23, Gal. 5:1). It is unjust for one brother to "judge" [lit., sharply criticize or condemn] his brother based on private convictions. It is the Lord who makes us stand (14:4), not one another; to "stand" means to be justified (recall 5:1–2). If God justifies a person, it is irrelevant who else does or does not justify him (recall 8:33).

"Each person must be convinced in his own mind" (14:5)—that is, concerning opinions. The context here does not concern different interpretations of doctrine but matters not specifically defined by doctrine. You have your convictions about certain foods, holidays, recreational pursuits, music tastes, etc., and I have mine; each one of us must be "convinced" that what we do (or partake of) is done to the glory of God ("for the Lord"). However, I cannot force my personal convictions upon you, nor can you judge me because I do not share your private convictions. The word of God should already condition such convictions—i.e., *no* conviction is justifiable which violates the attitude or behavior of Christ (Phil. 2:5, 1 John 2:4–6).

I do not live for you, nor do you live for me; we who are in Christ live "for the Lord" (14:7–12). This cannot mean that it does not matter what we believe, nor can it mean that we do not consider one another in what we do (recall 12:9–10; see Phil. 2:3–4). Rather, it means that our Master is Christ, and He measures our work, not someone else (or even our own convictions). God is the One who approves us based upon our faith in Him (2 Cor. 10:17–18, Heb. 11:1–2); this approval does not rest upon conformity to others' preferences or personal convictions. Christ did not die and rise from the dead just so that we could judge each other; He did these things so that we might live to Him (14:9). Paul uses the "stand" concept both as an encouragement and a warning: it is the Lord who makes us stand (14:4), but we will all stand before Christ (God) in the judgment (14:10; see 2 Cor. 5:10). The idea is: if we attempt to "stand" on our own convictions (i.e., by using them as a test of Christian fellowship) rather than on Christ, then it will not go well for us when we "stand" in the judgment.

Seeking Peace, Not Creating Division (14:13–23): Instead of critiquing and condemning other Christians' personal convictions, the "strong" are to refrain from putting such stumbling blocks before the weak (14:13). An "obstacle" is any kind of unnecessary hindrance; "stumbling block" is a trap or snare, something deliberately laid down in one's path to trip him up (i.e., to cause him to sin against his conscience).[194] Jesus used strong language against those who would cause others to stumble (Mat. 13:41, 18:1–11, and Luke 17:1). Two Christians may have completely different convictions about what is proper to eat, for example, yet both can be justified by faith in God. On this subject, Paul knows that eating meat (specifically, meat that is sacrificed to an idol; see 1 Cor. 10:24–33) is not unlawful, since "nothing is unclean in itself" (14:14; see Mark 7:18–19, 1 Tim. 4:1–5). However, Paul would not exercise this Christian liberty of his if it caused another Christian to violate his conscience: he would refrain from eating meat in the company of one who (because of his lack of knowledge) believed it would be sinful to do so.[195] "Do not destroy with your food"—or with any other matter of personal opinion—"him for whom Christ died" (14:15; see 1 Cor. 8:9–13).

This entire section (14:1–23) certainly speaks of Christian liberties: where they exist and where (or when) they must be set aside. One's Christian liberty is a "good thing" but can be "spoken of as evil [lit., blasphemed]" if not exercised properly (14:16). The spiritual matters of God's kingdom must be more important than one's personal preferences, liberties, or opinions (14:17). Being "acceptable" to God must be more important than being self-approved (14:18); being "approved by men"—i.e., having a good reputation among the brethren—must be more important than imposing one's private convictions upon another. "[T]he things which make for peace" (14:19) refers to those attitudes and behaviors that "preserve the unity of the Spirit" (Eph. 4:3; see Heb. 12:14). The "building up of one another" refers to edification, which is the responsibility of every Christian (1 Thess. 5:14–15), since "all things [are to be] done for edification" (1 Cor. 14:26). Not everything lawful is automatically edifying; not everything permissible is always wise or compassionate (1 Cor. 10:23–24). We are to be sensitive to the limited knowledge and tender consciences of those who are weak in faith.

God's "work" in a believer is far too important to "tear down" or jeopardize because of human convictions about far lesser things (14:20–21). At the same time, something can be "clean" or permissible to one person but violates the conscience of another. "The faith which you have…" (14:22)—this obviously cannot be *the* faith, as in the gospel of Christ (Jude 1:3). Paul is not saying, "Whatever doctrine you choose to believe (or, *however* you choose to believe it) makes no difference to God," for he is dealing here with private opinions and expendable liberties, not theology. Rather, he means: "What you do in faith, believing that it is to the glory of God, do it with full conviction and do not violate it." This does not mean one's beliefs cannot change, but that God recognizes that person's faith in Him for what it is and will accept it. Barrett translates 14:22b as follows: "Blessed is he who does not waver in respect of what his conscience affirms," which helps us to understand the meaning there.[196] One who knows what is wrong *for him* but partakes of it anyway violates his conscience and is self-condemned (14:23). Yet, one is "happy," or "blessed," or approved by God, if what he does agrees with his conscience—as long as his conscience itself is in agreement with God's law.

The "Strong" and "Weak" Are to Work Together (15:1–13): Paul's message to the "strong"—those who are to "accept the one who is weak in faith" (14:1)—continues into chapter 15. "Strong" (15:1) does not mean humanly superior, but learned, spiritually mature, "trained to discern good and evil" (Heb. 5:14), and having knowledge tempered with love (1 Cor. 8:1–3). The strong Christian has a moral responsibility to conduct himself appropriately toward the weak(er) Christian. This does not mean the strong can never advise, re-direct, or even reprove the weak; rather, he is not to be concerned only with his own views but is to consider his brother's convictions and sensitivities as well. But such respect and deference are to be mutual: "Each of us" indicates an action taken on both sides of the relationship (15:2). Thus, it is the responsibility of the weak to imitate and learn from those who are strong in the Lord (1 Cor. 11:1, Heb. 13:7). Being weak ought to be a phase, not a career; every Christian begins as a weak Christian, but none of us should ever be content to remain one. Historically, it is the "untaught and unstable" who often distort Scripture, not the strong (2 Peter 3:16).[197] Thus, the implied admonition to the weak is warranted.

As always, "edification" is the goal (15:2): the building up of one another in love (1 Cor. 14:26b and Eph. 4:16). The strong Christian's attitude of "pleasing" his fellow believer—not gratifying his every *request* but accommodating his immature *faith*—follows Christ's example who did this for all of us, strong and weak alike. No one is strong apart from Christ, and all of us are weak in comparison to Him; therefore, the Lord sees us all as equals (15:3; citation is from Psalm 69:9). Having just cited from the OT, Paul then explains that such things were written and preserved so that "we might have hope" (15:4).[198] The "hope" here refers to the fact that if we practice those things which are of heavenly origin, we will enjoy positive results.

The fact that we all are equal in God's sight, all share the same hope, and all read the same inspired Scripture, means that we can glorify God with "one voice [or mouth]" (15:6). We cannot do this, however, if we are not of the "same mind" (15:6; see 1 Cor. 1:10, Phil. 1:27, and 2:1–5). The many NT passages that speak to the *unity* of God's word, God's people, and what God's people do (together), make it impossible to justify religious divisions among us and still claim to be in good standing with Him. On the other hand, we can all have the "same mind" whether we are strong or weak: the power of Christ and His unifying gospel can accomplish this among all those who submit to Him.

We cannot be of "one accord" if fractured or divided, or if we refuse to "accept one another" (15:7). Again, Paul cites the humble yet sublime example of Christ to explain what this means. Christ, having been a "servant to the circumcision [i.e., Jews]" was also a servant "for the Gentiles": He has united both groups into one body (the church), all to the glory of God (Eph. 2:11–18). He has "confirm[ed] the promises given to Israel" (15:8), to which God has always been faithful (see Josh. 21:45, for example). His benevolent mercy has also become the source of tremendous praise among the Gentiles (15:9–11). Salvation comes by way of Israel but is gladly received by all nations (the OT quotes are, in order, from Psalm 18:49, Deut. 32:43, and Psalm 117:1).[199] The "root of Jesse" (15:12) refers to Christ's fulfillment of the promise given to David, Jesse's son, by which both Jews and Gentiles are blessed (citation is from Isa. 11:10).[200]

Since Christ has done so much on our behalf, the strong have no excuse to promote personal convictions or agendas at the expense of a fellow brother in the Lord. Likewise, no weaker brother has any right to use his weakness as a means of taking selfish advantage of those who are trying to show him love and concern. "Now may the God of hope fill you with all joy …" (15:13)—Paul has said a great deal about "hope" in this epistle (recall 5:1–5, 8:24–25, 12:12, and 15:4). Hope is one of the supreme benefits of a righteous life with God; one who believes in God may "abound in hope" because of the "power of the Holy Spirit." The Spirit gives life and meaning to one's hope in a future life with God: one sanctified by God's Spirit has every reason to experience joy and peace.

A Proper Regard for Paul's Ministry (15:14–33)

Paul's Ministry to the Gentiles (15:14–21): Paul spoke highly of the Roman Christians; his letter does not seem to deal with any specific problem among them (15:14–15).[201] Regardless, God commissioned him to speak with apostolic authority concerning His doctrine. He thus spoke boldly and unapologetically, as we see in this section. "Why should one write timidly to people who are full of goodness and of knowledge? They are the very ones to whom one may speak frankly and daringly. Their goodness will not draw wrong conclusions, and their knowledge will help them to understand."[202] Even though such information may only be a reminder to those who hear it, it is still important (cf. 2 Peter 1:12–15, 3:1–2).

Paul took his work among the Gentiles seriously and did not want such effort to be in vain (Gal. 2:2, 4:11, etc.). In fact, he likens himself to a public servant ("minister")[203] and then to a priest offering up a living and holy sacrifice to God ("ministering"), the Gentiles being that offering (15:16; see Isa. 66:20). "[S]anctified by the Holy Spirit" indicates that God has given divine approval to this ministry (Eph. 3:1–11). While he is proud of his own accomplishments in this ministry, Paul defers all glory to God (15:17–18). It is His "signs and wonders"—i.e., divine proofs—that give credibility to his ministry (2 Cor. 12:12).

As a result of Paul's extraordinary efforts, many Jews and Gentiles have heard and obeyed the gospel, from Jerusalem into Illyricum, a Roman province north of Macedonia (also known as Dalmatia). (While we have no record in Acts of him going into Illyricum, Paul's statement here is every bit as credible as Luke's record in Acts.) In every opportunity, he "fully preached the gospel of Christ," which is "the whole purpose of God" (Acts 20:27). He was often a trailblazer and a planter, establishing churches where others had not, rather than building on the work of others (15:20–21; see 1 Cor. 3:5–9). The church in Rome was an exception to this, but Paul realized the far-reaching benefits of having a church of God succeed in one of the major hubs of the ancient world. The citation in 15:21 (from Isa. 52:15) speaks paradoxically to the greatness of a crucified King. "The design of quoting it is to justify the principle on which the apostle acted. It was revealed that the gospel should be preached to the Gentiles; and he regarded it as a high honour [sic] to be the instrument of carrying this prediction into effect."[204]

The Gentiles' Indebtedness to the Jews (15:22–33): "For this reason..." (15:22)—i.e., Paul here explains why he has not yet visited the church in Rome. He has been extremely busy traveling; he has had a great deal of work to do; and he has a mission to take care of (detailed shortly). His delay was not for lack of desire but lack of time; also, difficult circumstances have hindered him from seeing these brethren (recall 1:11–13; cf. 1 Thess. 2:18). Having done what he could do in "these regions" (i.e., where he had already preached the gospel and established churches), he anticipated moving on to further regions (15:23).

Paul's immediate concern, however, is the collection of benevolence money from (predominantly) Gentile churches for the saints in Jerusalem (15:25–27). Paul did not say why the Jewish Christians were in such need, but there are legitimate reasons:

- Famine had hit several parts of the Roman Empire—and especially Palestine—during the reign of Emperor Claudius (AD 41–54).
- Christians in Jerusalem faced persecution from non-believing Jews there, which could have hindered employment and other opportunities enjoyed by the Jewish community.
- Families may have divided over the gospel (as Jesus predicted in Mat. 10:34–36), leaving some members without any financial support.
- The gospel attracts the poor and ostracized, as it continues to do today; these people may look to the church for their only means of support.

Paul admits an ulterior motive for this collection as well. He hopes to draw the Gentile and Jewish churches together, forcing them to realize how indebted they are to one another (see 1 Cor. 9:11 [in principle], and 2 Cor. 8:12–15). In receiving this gift from the Gentiles, the Jews could not accuse Paul of abandoning them, or claim that the Gentiles had no concern for their Jewish brethren.[205] The Macedonians' generosity is detailed in 2 Cor. 8:1–5: out of their own poverty, they did what they could to send money to Jerusalem. "Achaia" alludes to the Corinthians, who procrastinated in their original pledge to help, but (apparently) did ultimately provide financial assistance, at Paul's urging.

Once this money was delivered to the elders in Jerusalem (Acts 21:15–17), it is Paul's intention to travel to Spain in yet another missionary journey, stopping briefly in Rome on the way.[206] (Spain at this time was under Roman jurisdiction, and encompassed the entire Iberian Peninsula, which includes modern-day Spain and Portugal.) He is aware, however, that he has many enemies in Jerusalem, and anticipates trouble (15:30–33). Indeed, the Spirit has promised him "bonds and afflictions" there (see Acts 20:22–24); thus, he requests prayers on his behalf (as in Eph. 6:18–20 and Col. 4:2–4).

Paul may have had no idea of the full extent of what would happen to him in Jerusalem. He will be arrested on false charges and spend some two years in Roman custody awaiting a fair trial. Unable to get such a trial in Jerusalem or Caesarea, he would appeal to Caesar (Acts 25:10–12). Thus, he would indeed come to Rome, but as a prisoner in chains, not as the free man that he was at the time he wrote this epistle. This must have been a humiliating experience for Paul—not only to be treated as a criminal, but for his imprisonment to be the Roman Christians' first actual glimpse of him.[207]

Paul's Greetings and Final Admonitions (16:1–27)

Ancient letters often included the author's "commendation" or personal endorsement of the one who carried it (see 2 Cor. 3:1). In the present case, Paul commends a Christian lady named Phoebe for this purpose (16:1–2). Phoebe was apparently a woman of some prominence, possibly a well-to-do widow, and is referred to in the Greek text as a deaconess [lit., *diakonos*, often translated here as "servant"].[208] Indeed, she had served in the role of a helper and servant, and Paul gives high praise to her for this reason. Cenchrea is an ancient port town in Achaia a few miles east of Corinth (Acts 18:18), where *Romans* is believed to have been penned.

Paul's Salutations to Various Brethren (16:3–16): This section is the longest list of greetings in the NT. Prisca and Aquila (16:3–4) are undoubtedly the same Priscilla and Aquila from Acts 18:1–3 and 18:24–26. Paul's last known epistle also mentions this faithful couple (2 Tim. 4:19). They had rescued Paul from a life-threatening situation to their own endangerment. This sparing of Paul's life made it possible for him to bring the gospel message to many Gentiles. Notice in 16:5a that "the church" (i.e., a local congregation of believers) met in this couple's home, which is how most early Christians assembled for worship—in private homes, not church buildings.

There is little or nothing known about the rest of these people, except that their names are often of Latin or Greek origin. Likely, these people were either Gentiles or Hellenized (Greek-cultured) Jews; many may have been, like Paul, Roman citizens. It is obvious that Paul was well-traveled to have known so many people, and that he had friends all over the known world. "Rufus" (16:13) may be the one mentioned in Mark 15:21, the son of Simon of Cyrene who bore Jesus' cross; however, aside from the common name, there is little else upon which to base this.

The custom of greeting with a kiss (16:16) was common in the ancient world and continues in some countries today. This form of greeting compares to a handshake in our own American or Western European culture. The emphasis seems not to be on the practice itself (i.e., this is not a command to literally kiss one another) but speaks of the nature of it: the "kiss" is to be a holy one, not one given in deceit (think of Judas' kiss of betrayal) or with impropriety (see 1 Tim. 2:8 for a parallel idea). In other words, whatever form of greeting we use ought to be with genuineness and holiness, not with hypocrisy or ungodly motives.

The phrase "churches of Christ" (16:16) appears nowhere else in the NT. Paul uses "church [or churches] of God" with far more frequency—eleven times in all. In several cases, Christ's churches are identified by where they are: "the church of God which is at Corinth" (1 Cor. 1:2, 2 Cor. 1:1); "the church which is at Cenchrea" (Rom. 16:1); "the church of the Laodiceans" (Col. 4:16); "the church of the Thessalonians" (1 Thess. 1:1, 2 Thess. 1:1); etc. Such expressions are descriptive, not authoritative: they define groups of people with a common identity and in a common locale. The phrase "church of Christ" is not a name, nor a formal, official, or denominational title for Christ's churches. Indeed, the spiritual body of Christ is not comprised of churches (congregations), but only of individual members. The brotherhood may use "churches of Christ" today to identify congregations with a common belief system; however, there is no authority to use this name alone as a test of fellowship for those who use another biblically acceptable name.

Paul closes this epistle with a strong admonition to "keep your eyes on those who cause dissensions and hindrances contrary to the teaching which you learned, and turn away from them" (16:17). His objective is to promote "the bond of peace in the unity of the Spirit" (Eph. 4:3; recall 14:19); those who undermine that unity are divisive (1 Cor. 1:10–13). "The man who causes divisions in the Lord's church by the introduction of things not taught is an enemy of Christ, even though he may not think so."[209] "Hindrance" [Greek, *skandalon*] is translated elsewhere as "offense" or "stumbling block": divisive people create a satanic obstacle to Christian fellowship (see Phil. 3:18–19). For this reason, they are to be "marked" or identified; their agenda is a self-serving and deceptive one, regardless of what they profess (16:18).[210]

There are, in every congregation, "the unsuspecting [or, innocent]"—those who are still tender and naïve toward the stratagems and manipulations of false teachers (2 Peter 2:18–19). Thus, while he rejoices over their success, Paul warns the Roman Christians not to become complacent toward or oblivious to danger (16:19). God's people are to be wise in what is good, not well-acquainted with evil; they are to be aware of danger, but not participating in dangerous activities that threaten their souls (Mat. 10:16, 1 Cor. 14:20). "The God of peace will soon crush Satan under your feet" (16:20)—whether this is a prophetic disclosure (as in Gen. 3:15 or 2 Tim. 4:3–5) or simply one based upon biblical history, the statement is true. God's people will be victorious over Satan if they choose God over any other source of deliverance (James 4:7–8).

Finally, Paul includes greetings from those who are traveling with him (16:21–23; cf. Acts 20:1–5). These names are also either Greek or Latin in origin; these people may have had ties to Rome or were personally acquainted with Roman Christians. "Timothy" is undoubtedly the same protégé of Paul's to whom *1 & 2 Timothy* were written; he is likely also the one who was later imprisoned (Heb. 13:23). "Jason" may have been the same man mentioned in Acts 17:5–9, and "Sosipater" may be the Sopater of Acts 20:4, but we cannot substantiate these conclusions.

"Tertius" was the *amanuensis* (i.e., a copyist or secretary) who penned this epistle at Paul's dictation; Paul honors him by allowing his personal greeting. "Gaius" may be the one mentioned in 1 Cor. 1:14, not the man from Derbe (Acts 20:4); whether he is the Gaius from John's epistles is unknown to us for certain, but it seems unlikely, given the span of time between the two epistles, and because Gaius was a very common name in Paul's day. "Erastus" was the "city treasurer"—i.e., of the city of Corinth—which indicates how deeply the gospel had penetrated through various social strata in that place. "Quartus" [Latin, "the fourth"] is unknown to us. Many scholars do not even acknowledge 16:24, as it is not in any of the earliest manuscripts; its redundancy (from 16:20b) is also conspicuous. Nonetheless, the content of this verse is neither contradictory nor questionable.

Paul fittingly closes this profound letter with a doxology—a hymn of praise to God (16:25–27). He condenses several important points that are expounded upon elsewhere:

- ❑ **"He who is able to establish you"**—God the Father is the source of one's grounding and stability through Jesus Christ and His Holy Spirit (2 Cor. 1:21, Heb. 13:20–21, and 1 Peter 5:10). God—really, the Godhead (the Father, Son, and Holy Spirit)—is deeply concerned with and involved in the establishment of every soul that belongs to Him.
- ❑ **"according to my gospel"**—recall 2:16; see Eph. 1:13–14 and Col. 1:23.

Christ recognizes no gospel other than the one which He gave to Paul to preach (Acts 26:16–18); to preach a "different" gospel warrants a divine curse (Gal. 1:8).

- **"the preaching of Jesus Christ"**—see Acts 8:35, 1 Cor. 2:1–5, and 2 Cor. 4:5. Any gospel that is not centered entirely upon the character and redemptive work of Christ the Redeemer is not from God. Such gospels may have "the appearance of wisdom in self-made religion" (Col. 2:23), but they are of no value in attaining righteousness from God.
- **"according to the revelation of the mystery"**—see Eph. 3:1–12, Col. 2:1–2, and 1 Tim. 3:16. Whenever Paul mentions a "mystery," he also speaks of its having been "revealed": the gospel is indeed God's divine revelation to man, first in the bodily form of Jesus Christ (John 1:14, Heb. 1:1–3), then in the words of His apostles (Heb. 2:1–4).
- **"and by the Scriptures of the prophets"**—see Luke 24:25–27, Acts 3:18, 17:3–4, and 2 Peter 3:1–2. The gospel of Christ is built upon and grew out of the promises and prophecies proclaimed by Moses and the Prophets. Thus, the gospel is not in contradiction to the Law (of Moses) but a fulfillment of it (see Acts 24:14–15).
- **"according to the commandment"**—see John 12:50, 1 Thess. 4:2, and 1 John 2:25. Paul himself spoke the gospel of Christ "according to the commandment of God" (1 Tim. 1:1); Christ's own high-priestly office was established by a divine oath (Heb. 7:17–22). Whatever God does *for* people is the result of His *command*.
- **"has been made known ... nations"**—see Mat. 28:19, Acts 1:8, and Col. 1:5–6,23. Because of the Holy Spirit's oversight and the tenacious evangelism of early Christians, the gospel quickly permeated the entire known world by the end of the first century.
- **"the obedience of faith"**—recall 1:5 and 15:18; see also Acts 6:7. Faith in God necessarily requires obedience to God's commandments (1 John 2:4–6). Even Jesus was not above the law; His worthiness was the result of His infallible obedience to God's commands (Heb. 5:8–9). While our obedience will not be perfect as Christ's was, our respect for God's commands and our attitude toward obedience must imitate His.

Paul ends this beautiful doxology with this: "To the only wise God, through Jesus Christ, be the glory forever. Amen." The "wisdom of God" is infinitely greater than the wisdom of men (1 Cor. 1:18–29); this wisdom comes through the unparalleled teachings of His Son, Jesus Christ.

Appendix: Calvinism (a.k.a. Doctrine of Predestination)

Calvinism (a.k.a. Reformed Theology, Doctrine of Predestination, or Doctrine of Election and Reprobation) is a particular interpretation of Scripture and salvation in which God's sovereignty determines the salvation (election) or condemnation (reprobation) of every single human soul. Augustine (343—430) popularized this view, but John Calvin (1509—1564) formally articulated it. Since so much of the alleged defense for this doctrine comes from *Romans*, it seemed necessary to expound upon it at least briefly.[211]

On the surface, Calvinism appears as a noble and humble tribute to the righteousness of God. It maintains that God's sovereignty cannot be overruled by any human decision—which, by itself, is a true and biblical statement. The problem begins in how Calvinism applies this truth in the context of salvation. It maintains that no one can resist God's saving grace: if God intends to save you, then you *must* be saved. Calvinism also maintains that a person is not just blinded by his sin (citing 2 Cor. 4:3–4) but is *literally* dead to God's gospel call (citing Eph. 2:1). Since a person is dead to God, it is impossible for him to respond; since he cannot respond, it is up to God to revive him. This leaves the decision to be *made alive* or *left for dead* God's and His alone. Thus, no one can have faith in the gospel of Christ who has not first been "made alive" (regenerated) by God first.

This view turns Paul's argument concerning faith on its head: instead of a person being credited with righteousness because of his faith (Rom. 1:17, 4:3), Calvinism teaches that a person cannot practice faith until he has first been regenerated by God. Instead of God's grace being a response to man's faith, Calvinism teaches that a person's faith is a compelled response to God's grace. Furthermore, one is not "born again" after hearing the word of God (because he remains "dead") but God must *make* him "born again" first—regardless of that person's awareness of this. Once "made alive," a person *then* can respond rightly to God's commands for repentance, holy living, and good works.[212]

According to Calvinism, a person is "dead" as the direct result of Adam's sin (a.k.a. the Doctrine of Original Sin).[213] When Adam sinned, he "killed" the family of humanity regarding people's ability to obey God's truth. In this condition, allegedly one has *permission* to come to God, but he *cannot* come because he is "dead."

> ... All people are conceived in sin and born children of wrath, unfit for any saving good, inclined to evil, dead in their sins, and slaves to sin; [and] without the grace of the regenerating Holy Spirit they are neither willing nor able to return to God, to reform their distorted nature, or even to dispose themselves to such reform.[214]

God will punish all those not called by His grace; those called by God's grace will escape all condemnation. Thus, according to Calvinism, some human souls ("reprobates") will be eternally lost because they have incurred Adam's guilt for his sins and thus God's condemnation (regardless of their own sins). All other human souls ("the elect") are saved because God decided, by His sovereign authority, to redeem them from the condemnation of Adam's guilt (regardless of their own faith, repentance, or obedience to God).[215]

Naturally, Calvinists will cite Scripture to support this doctrine. Below are some of the most common passages cited. (The brief summaries after each citation are their own interpretations.)

- ❑ John 6:44, no one can come to God unless He first regenerates that person.
- ❑ Acts 13:48, no one can have eternal life whom God did not "appoint" beforehand.
- ❑ Rom. 3:10–18, no one does any "good" without God's having first regenerated him.
- ❑ Rom. 8:29–30, God "predestines" whomever He will; those whom He has not predestined are eternally lost. No one can dispute God's having not called him, since His sovereign authority is not to be questioned.
- ❑ Rom. 9:10–18, God "calls" whomever He wishes, and does not "call" whomever He chooses not to call. Thus, God called Jacob, but "hated" Esau; God called the Israelites but did not call Pharaoh. (This all assumes that Paul was talking about the *eternal disposition* of Jacob's, Esau's, and Pharaoh's souls, which he was not—MY WORDS.)
- ❑ Eph. 1:3–11 (and every passage which speaks of God's "choosing" His people, His "choice," or the "elect"), God has "predestined" those who are saved; thus, He has *not* predestined those who will be lost. The entire matter rests in God's own decision; a person can only accept whatever sovereign decree He has made concerning him.

- Eph. 2:1–2, man is "dead" in sin, and thus is unable to respond to God's gospel until God makes him "alive" in Christ (2:4–5).
- Eph. 2:8–9, human "works" play no part in his salvation, but he is saved by divine grace alone. "Faith" is what a person gives to God after He has saved him.

The above citations do not prove Calvinism, but instead are "interpreted" in light of it. This is like an evolutionist "proving" evolution with fossils that he claims are the result of evolution! Such circular reasoning does not create a valid argument, but only spins around an idea (like a dog chasing its tail) without ever proving anything. The context of each passage, and of the entire NT, simply does not support the interpretations that Calvinism has assigned to it.

When Paul speaks of "predestination" (as in Rom. 8:29–30 or Eph. 1:5–12), he always does so in reference to the entire body of believers, not individual people. In other words, Christ's *church* is predestined for salvation and glory, but it is left up to each individual person to determine whether he will be *part* of that church, based upon his *own response* to the gospel (Mat. 7:13–14, John 3:36, 8:24, Rom. 10:9–10, etc.). The NT repeatedly and consistently teaches that the *free will to choose* salvation (or remain in condemnation) remains with the one who has sinned against God. While it *is* God's sovereign will to provide this salvation—and it *is* His "desire" for every person to be saved (1 Tim. 2:4)—it is *also* His sovereign will to leave the decision *of* salvation up to the individual sinner.

If people are saved independent of, and even regardless of, their own free will, then this leaves the fate of their eternal souls completely in God's hands. This is what Calvinism wants to say, but this always favors the Calvinist and assumes that anyone who *is* a Calvinist is, of course, one of the "elect" and not one of the "reprobates." In other words, Calvinism necessarily teaches that God will send an untold number of souls to hell *not* because they rejected Him, but because *He* rejected *them* and inexplicably refused to save them. In sharp contrast, Paul says that God's wrath will be the result of a person's wicked "deeds," and one's righteousness will be credited to him only because he sought to obey the truth and do good (Rom. 2:4–11).

Calvinists are fond of citing "God's sovereign will"—something unknown and incomprehensible to us, they say—to make sense of their doctrine. Yet, the only way anyone can *know* "God's sovereign will" is for Him to have *revealed* it; otherwise, we cannot *cite* a "will" of God's that He never revealed that contradicts what He *did* reveal. The NT does not rest upon unknown factors, mysterious information, and unexplained doctrine. On the contrary, everything that God wanted us to know, He revealed; and what He revealed does not support Calvinism but refutes it.

Calvinists are also fond of appealing to church history as justification for their beliefs. Thus, they regularly cite the various religious councils (a.k.a. synods) in which landmark decisions have been rendered by a high court of church officials. In some of these councils, Calvinism has been exonerated, while those who oppose it are summarily condemned as heretics. Two of these so-called heretics—Pelagius (354—420?) and James Arminius (1560—1609)—are identified as "founders" of modern anti-Calvinistic teachings. Thus, Calvinists call non-Calvinists who identify as Christians "Pelagians," "semi-Pelagians," or "Arminians." This, of course, assumes that all such non-Calvinists are in full agreement with all that these men taught—a point which is neither true nor necessary.[216]

In bold response to James Arminius' remonstrance or formal grievance against Calvinism, Calvinists convened a historic council in the city of Dordrecht, Netherlands—commonly referred to as Dort (or Dordt)—from 1618 to 1619. In this council, Calvinists outlined a five-point statement of their beliefs, mnemonically referred to as "TULIP."[217]

- ☐ **Total Hereditary Depravity:** Since man's heart, emotions, will, mind, and body are completely affected by Adam's sin, he is born sinful and thus condemned. He is "dead" in his sins, and thus unable to respond to God's gospel.
  - This must mean, then, that Jesus was also born sinful, since He is the Son of Man ("born of a woman"—Gal. 4:4) as well as the Son of God. This must also mean that all babies and young children are also born sinful and will suffer punishment for actions for which they cannot possibly be held responsible. (Calvinists explain that those who die as infants or children may be "called" by God without us knowing it, so that their souls are saved.)
  - Calvinists take Paul's "dead" reference (in Eph. 2:1) quite literally, but never really explain what, exactly, is "dead." If it is a person's *soul*, then how can he function as a living being? If it is his *spiritual awareness*, then how can he have any consciousness? If it is his *relationship* (or fellowship) with God, this makes sense[218]—but the

Calvinist wants it to mean so much more than this. The NT teaches: a person is dead (or "fallen"—Rom. 3:23), but this refers to his ability to walk in fellowship with God. Yet he can respond to God's gospel, for God has made it available to him for this very purpose (Rom. 10:5–13). If a person can "call upon the name of the Lord," then he most certainly can take the initiative regarding his salvation (Acts 2:21, 22:16).

- **Unconditional Election:** God does not base His "election" upon anything He sees in an individual person. He is unconcerned with what men do or do not do. He saves (or does not save) based solely upon His sovereign decision.
  - This is a complete distortion of the meaning of "sovereignty of God." There is no question that it is God who regenerates the human soul, or that His grace—the atonement of Christ and the power of His Spirit—is the means of that regeneration (John 1:12–13, Titus 3:4–7, 1 Peter 1:2, etc.). But to place the full responsibility upon God for whether this regeneration takes place (and thus to deny man's free will) makes God a "respecter of persons" and a God of partiality—exactly the opposite of what the Bible teaches (Acts 10:34–35, Rom. 2:11, Eph. 6:9, and Col. 3:25). If God justifies a person based upon his faith in Him, then He would be an unjust God to deny him that opportunity for which Christ has died (John 12:32, 20:31).
  - To allow a person his free, independent will to choose this opportunity or refuse it is not questioning God's decision. His gospel stands intact, whether one chooses to obey it; His sovereignty remains unchallenged, whether one chooses to acknowledge it. It is conspicuous, too, that everyone who supports Calvinism is conveniently part of the "elect," and thus has no problem upholding God's decision to save them. This strongly indicates religious bias and conflict of interest. One loses all objectivity in interpreting Scripture when he believes that he cannot be wrong in his interpretation—and cannot be lost no matter what.
- **Limited Atonement:** "Jesus died only for the elect. Though Jesus' sacrifice was sufficient for all, it was not efficacious for all. Jesus only bore the sins of the elect."[219]
  - This is based upon statements like Isa. 53:12 and Mat. 26:28, where it says Jesus died for "many" but not "all." It is also based upon John 17:9, where Jesus prayed only for His disciples, but not for "the world." It is clear to any objective Bible student that when one uses

passages like these in such a restrictive manner, they will only work for the one who so interprets them but no one else.

- God sent Jesus to die for the entire world (John 3:16, 1 John 2:2). Just because the entire world does not rightly respond to His death does not mean that He did not die for all people. Passages that assert that Jesus died "for many" and not "all" cannot be construed to mean that Jesus' death was ineffectual for those not included in the "many," but that only those ("many") who do call upon His name for salvation will be atoned by His blood. They do not restrict His work on the cross but only concede that not all will appreciate that work.

❏ **Irresistible Grace:** "When God calls His elect into salvation, they cannot resist. God offers to all people the gospel message. This is called the external call. But to the elect, God extends an internal call and it cannot be resisted."[220] Being "born again" is just like physical birth: the one being born has no part in the decision to be born.

- The above conclusion misunderstands and misapplies what is taught in Scripture. In Phil. 2:12–13, for example, it says "God … is at work in you," which is straightforward enough. It does not mean, "God chooses salvation for you," but that God does things for the believer that he cannot do for himself. This is called grace, but it is not irresistible. People can receive grace "in vain" (2 Cor. 6:1–2); they can turn away from the Spirit of grace (Heb. 10:26–29). Paul warned the Galatians that they were in danger of falling from grace (Gal. 5:4)—one cannot "fall" from something he never had in the first place.
- The truth is that people can and do resist God's grace. This does not undermine God's sovereignty but is a refusal of what His sovereign decisions have offered them. God's commandment is eternal life (John 12:30); but not everyone chooses to obey this command (Heb. 4:2). This does not make Him any less "God"; it only makes those who refuse Him foolish people.
- "Born again" in the spiritual sense is an analogy, not a literal replication of one's physical birth. While it is true that I did not choose to be physically born, it is not true that my spiritual rebirth is held to this same condition. One is biological, the other is spiritual; one is natural, the other is supernatural; one regards my human (earthly) existence, the other regards my spiritual (eternal) existence. The two "births" may share some common features but are not identical or interchangeable. Calvinists conspicuously avoid

John 3:5: "Unless one is born of water and the Spirit..." Being born of the Spirit is what God does for believer; being born of water is what the believer does for God, in faithful obedience to what He has commanded. It is not only necessary that the believer participate in his born-again experience, but he is expected to initiate it through his baptism.

- **Perseverance of the Saints:** "You cannot lose your salvation. Because the Father has elected, the Son has redeemed, and the Holy Spirit has applied salvation, those thus saved are eternally secure." Jesus said in John 10:27–28 that His "sheep" cannot perish; Paul said in Rom. 8:1 that the believer has passed out of condemnation; see also 1 Cor. 10:13 and Phil. 1:6.
    - This point disregards the conditional premise of each passage being considered. God promises to never leave us (Heb. 13:5), but this does not mean we cannot leave Him (Heb. 6:4–8). Jesus will present every believer before the Father, but only if that person will "continue in the faith firmly established and steadfast, and not moved away from the hope of the gospel that you have heard" (Col. 1:21–23).
    - Calvinists also wrestle with passages like Rom. 11:22, which necessitate this conditional situation. Calvinists like to make God's decree the "condition," but Paul clearly teaches that man's faith is the variable. Paul (in Rom. 11:22) did not write to Gentiles who were guaranteed to be lost, but to those who had been saved: he warned them not to forfeit their salvation through unbelief. Thus, the burden is placed upon the believer to continue in his belief, not upon God to save someone regardless of his belief. God simply finalizes man's decision concerning his salvation; He does not make it unilaterally.
    - When someone does "fall away" from the faith, the Calvinist claims that that person was "never really saved at all," but only experienced "worldly sorrow" or a "dimension of enlightenment."[221] This theology is convenient, but not biblical. The NT teaches that not only *can* people fall away from the faith, but that some *will* (Acts 20:28–30, 1 Tim. 4:1, 2 Peter 2:20–22, etc.).

Calvinists cite passages from *Romans* to support their doctrine, but they do so sparingly and selectively. They wrestle, however, with passages (like Rom. 11:22) that necessitate the conditional factors regarding salvation. Calvinists like to make God's decree the "condition," but Paul clearly teaches that a person's faith is the variable. He warned Christians who had been saved not to forfeit their salvation through unbelief. Thus, the burden is placed upon the believer to continue in his belief, not upon God to save someone regardless of his belief. God simply finalizes each person's decision concerning his salvation; He does not make that decision unilaterally.

The NT teaches that one who is "dead" to God is not unable to respond to God's gospel, for God has made it available to him for this very purpose (Rom. 10:5–13). To place the full responsibility upon God for our salvation *or* condemnation both denies our free will and makes God a "respecter of persons"—the exact opposite of what the Bible teaches (Acts 10:34–35, Rom. 2:11, Eph. 6:9, and Col. 3:25).

Prayer, evangelism, good works, and benevolence are rendered pointless if indeed God is going to save whomever He wants regardless of what each person does or fails to do. The Calvinist will respond: first, the non-elected are *permitted* to come to God, just not *able*; second, since we do not know who the "elect" are, we are supposed to discover them through prayer and evangelism. Yet this smacks of arrogance and elitism, and these conclusions are plucked out of thin air. If *God's* will forces people to be saved against their *own* will, then they will be saved even without evangelism or prayer. And if we are forced to evangelize or pray or believe, then we are no longer intelligent human beings capable of free will but are merely automatons.

Calvinism is not just a harmless interpretation of Scripture; it is an imposing and damaging one. It misrepresents both God and His plan of salvation. Even though its supporters claim to honor God's sovereign will, they handcuff the *application* of His will to their own interpretations of it. Listening to their arguments, they place high confidence in their champions of biblical interpretation—chiefly, Augustine and John Calvin—but do not allow the Bible to speak for itself other than in its carefully dissected pieces. The apostle Paul was not a Calvinist, nor was Christ. Calvinism came long after the fact; it was not a part of what was taught to the early church.

Calvinism claims to be a valid expression of Christianity, but in fact it completely misrepresents the gospel of Christ—even though it claims to have the best of intentions—and makes huge, unwarranted, and even contradictory assumptions concerning God's will and the state of the human soul. It should be noted that, despite such glaring and irresolvable problems with this doctrine, it remains one of the most popular forms of

Christian theology today. Many of the major writers, contributors, and Q&A responders on the Internet are Calvinists (though rarely do they identify themselves as such). Likewise, many of the most popular Bible commentators being used today are also Calvinists.

It should not be our desire to defend what other people say about God and His salvation. Rather, it should be our earnest desire to believe, teach, and defend what God has said about Himself. This means that any responsible Christian should "[hold] fast the faithful word which is in accordance with the teaching, so that [we] will be able both to exhort in sound doctrine and to refute those who contradict" (Titus 1:9). Any doctrine that opposes the gospel of Christ deserves to be exposed for what it is: a "different gospel" (Gal. 1:6–8).

Sources Used for This Study

Barnes, Albert. *Barnes' Notes on the New Testament*, vol. 10. Database © 2014 by WORDsearch Corp. (orig. published by Blackie & Son, London, 1885).

Barrett, C. K. *The Epistle to the Romans*. New York: Harper & Row, 1957.

Bruce, F. F. "Romans, Epistle to the." *The Zondervan Pictorial Encyclopedia of the Bible*, vol. 5. Merrill C. Tenney, gen. ed. Grand Rapids: Zondervan Publishing, 1976.

Coffman, James Burton. *Commentary on Romans*. Austin, TX: Firm Foundation Publishing House, 1973.

Hendriksen, William. *New Testament Commentary: Exposition of Paul's Epistle to the Romans*. Grand Rapids: Baker Book House, 1981.

Hodge, Charles. *A Commentary on Romans*. Carlisle, PA: The Banner of Truth Trust, 1997 (orig. 1835).

Holman Bible Dictionary (electronic edition). Trent C. Butler, gen. ed. © 1991 by Holman Bible Publishers; database © 2008 by WORDsearch Corp.

Jamieson, Robert, A. R. Fausset, and David Brown. *Commentary Critical and Explanatory on the Whole Bible (1871)* (electronic edition). Database © 2012 by WORDsearch Corp.

Kelly, J. N. D. *The Pastoral Epistles*. Peabody, MA: Hendrickson Publishers, 1960.

Lard, Moses. *Commentary on Romans*. Delight, AR: Gospel Light Publishing Co., no date (orig. published 1863).

Lenski, R. C. H. *The Interpretation of St. Paul's Epistle to the Romans: Commentary on the New Testament*. Peabody, MA: Hendrickson Publishers, 1998.

Lipscomb, David. *A Commentary on the New Testament Epistles: Romans*. J. W. Shepherd, ed. Nashville, TN: Gospel Advocate Co., 1983.

Luther, Martin. *Commentary on Romans*. Translated by J. Theodore Mueller. Grand Rapids: Zondervan Publishing House, 1954.

McGuiggan, Jim. *The Book of Romans*. Lubbock, TX: Montex Publishing Co., 1982.

Miller, D. G. "Romans, Epistle to." *International Standard Bible Encyclopedia* (electronic edition) © 1979 by Wm. B. Eerdmans Publishing Co.; database © 2009 by WORDsearch Corp.

Robertson, A. T. *Word Pictures in the New Testament*, vol. 4 (electronic edition). © 1932, renewal © 1960, by the Sunday School Board of the Southern Baptist Convention; database © 2007 by WORDsearch Corp.

Schaff, Philip. *History of the Christian Church*, vol. VIII. Grand Rapids: Eerdmans Publishing Co., 1995.

Strong, James. *Strong's Talking Greek-Hebrew Dictionary* (electronic edition). Database © 2004 by WORDsearch Corp.

Teacher Bible Commentary (electronic edition). H. Franklin Paschall and Hershel H. Hobbs, eds. © 1972 by Broadman Press; database © 2009 by WORDsearch Corp.

Vincent, Marvin R. *Vincent's Word Studies in the New Testament*, vol. 3 (electronic edition). Database © 2014 by WORDsearch Corp.

Whiteside, R. L. *Commentary on Romans*. Denton, TX: Inys Whiteside, 1945.

Wuest, Kenneth S. *Word Studies in the Greek New Testament*, vol. 1. Grand Rapids: Eerdmans Publishing Co., 1955; reprinted, 1992.

Scripture taken from the NEW AMERICAN STANDARD BIBLE®, Copyright © 1960, 1962, 1963, 1968, 1971, 1972, 1973, 1975, 1977, 1995 by The Lockman Foundation. Used by permission.

Endnotes

1   Harold S. Songer, "Romans, Book of" *Holman Bible Dictionary* (electronic edition), Trent C. Butler, gen. ed. (© 1991 by Holman Bible Publishers; database © 2008 by WORDsearch Corp.).

2   D. G. Miller, "Romans, Epistle to," *International Standard Bible Encyclopedia* (electronic edition) (© 1979 by Wm. B. Eerdmans Publishing Co.; database © 2009 by WORDsearch Corp.).

3   Martin Luther, *Commentary on Romans*, trans. by J. Theodore Mueller (Grand Rapids: Zondervan Publishing House, 1954), xiii.

4   "Because Romans is the longest of Paul's letters and the most formal in structure, it has often been considered a formal theological treatise, intended as a compendium of Paul's theology to be preserved for posterity. For this reason, also, it has at times been neglected as a theoretical, impractical work, devoid of any relation to life" (Miller, "Romans," *ISBE* [electronic]). Yet, "if it is devoid of such [practical realities of life] we are faced with the inexplicable contradiction of a purely theoretical work coming up out of the life of one of the world's most practical men, at a time in his life when he was plotting the most magnificent practical task ever conceived by the human mind—to claim the entire world for Jesus Christ" (*Ibid.*, bracketed words are mine).

5   F. F. Bruce, "Romans, Epistles to the," *The Zondervan Pictorial Encyclopedia of the Bible*, vol. 5; Merrill C. Tenney, gen. ed. (Grand Rapids: Zondervan Publishing, 1976), 161; bracketed words are mine.

6   "Scholars generally agree that Paul's close relationship with the Corinthian church would have resulted in his staying there, and this is confirmed by Paul's mentioning that he was staying with Gaius (Rom. 16:23) who was a convert in Corinth (see 1 Cor. 1:14)" (Miller, "Romans," *ISBE* [electronic]).

7   For a thorough study on Paul's arrest and his subsequent trials, I recommend my *Acts Commentary* (Spiritbuilding Publishers, 2017); go to www.spiritbuilding.com/chad.

8   For a thorough study on grace, I strongly recommend my book, *The Gospel of Saving Grace* (Spiritbuilding Publishers, 2020); go to www.spiritbuilding.com/chad.

9   Calvinism teaches differently: "Our justification is by faith alone: works form no part of that righteousness in which we can stand before the tribunal

of God" (Charles Hodge, *A Commentary on Romans* [Carlisle, PA: The Banner of Truth Trust, 1997 (orig. 1835)], 32). According to Calvinism, God chooses who will be saved (and thus, who will not be saved) regardless of any works of faith: justification is by faith alone—and this "faith" is assumed to come even after a person is already "born again" and thus "saved" (see "Appendix"). Calvinism forces the word "alone" ("faith alone") into Paul's teaching because otherwise its explanation of salvation will not work. As it is, any doctrine is already invalidated by necessarily forcing words or teachings into the sacred text.

10   Luther says "'the flesh' is a man who lives and works, inwardly and outwardly, in the service of the flesh's profit and of this temporal life; 'the spirit' is the man who lives and works, inwardly and outwardly, in the service of the Spirit and the future life" (*Commentary*, xviii).

11   The Calvinistic view is very different than what Paul teaches. Paul says, in essence, "God credits a person with righteousness when he puts his faith in Him" (1:17, 4:3, etc.). Calvinism says that righteousness "is something done for us and imputed to us" (Hodge, *Commentary*, 31). This "imputed righteousness" concept means that Christ's own personal righteousness becomes our own personal righteousness. Just as sin is allegedly transferred from Adam to all who are born after him, so Christ's own righteousness is transferred to us. This takes faith (and human decision) out of the equation as a determinant of our standing before God. According to Calvinism, a person is justified by God before and even regardless of his faith in Him: having been "imputed" with Christ's righteousness, he cannot be lost, because Christ (whose righteousness is within him) cannot be lost; Christ's innocence becomes one's own innocence. But God does not "transfer" either guilt or righteousness. If one sins, it is because of that person's defiance against a righteous God; if one is forgiven, then it is because of that person's faith in a forgiving God. Christ demonstrated His own righteousness, and because of that flawless demonstration we can find atonement for our sins (1 Cor. 1:30). But this cannot be construed to mean that our personal responsibility for our sins has been absolved simply because He was righteous. Otherwise, the entire epistle of Romans—and in fact the entire New Testament—is pointless.

12   "The pivotal importance of understanding 'the righteousness of God' as God in action in Christ will only clearly be seen when it is grasped that the same Greek word root occurs in the terms translated into English as

righteousness, just, justification, and justify. Understanding what Paul meant by righteousness is therefore crucial for one's interpretation of Romans because it sets one's perception of justification as well" (Songer, "Romans," *Holman Bible Dictionary* [electronic]).

13 Some versions say "called {to be} an apostle," but the added words (in brackets) are unnecessary. "Paul was not merely called to be an apostle, as our common version has it; he was actually one" (Moses Lard, *Commentary on Romans* [Delight, AR: Gospel Light Publishing Co., orig. copyright 1863], 25).

14 Jeremiah uses the same expression concerning his own ministry (Jer. 1:5).

15 David Lipscomb, *A Commentary on the New Testament Epistles: Romans*, J. W. Shepherd, ed. (Nashville, TN: Gospel Advocate Co., 1983), 16.

16 "Spirit of holiness," while rendered "Holy Spirit" in some translations, is the correct phrase Paul uses here. Nonetheless, Paul does use "the Spirit of God" and "the Spirit of Christ" as interchangeable expressions of God's divine Spirit (as in Rom. 8:9; see 2 Cor. 3:17).

17 Lit., "holy (ones)" [Greek, *hagios*]. It is clear, however, that the word "saint" today carries a great deal of erroneous denominational baggage. For this reason, Moses Lard suggested: "The word 'saint' should be wholly dropped from the sacred page. It is too vague, and has been too much abused to be tolerated longer" (Lard, *Commentary*, 33). In my opinion, we should never drop any word from "the sacred page" just because one religious group or another has abused it. Rather, we should take every opportunity to provide the biblical and contextual usage of that word in hopes of correcting people's understanding of it.

18 "The fact that Paul did not speak of the 'church' in Rome may be significant; perhaps at this time there was no city-wide church in Rome with a community-consciousness of its own, as there was, for example, in Corinth, where Paul himself had planted and tended the church. On the other hand, the fact that Paul can address a letter to all the Christians in Rome implies some assurance on his part that they would all have access to it" (Bruce, "Romans," *Zondervan*, 148).

19 Of course, this visit did not happen in the way Paul intended. We know that he did go to Rome, but only upon his appeal to Caesar Nero (ca. AD 61–62) as a prisoner in chains. This shows that Paul did sometimes form his own plans apart from being directed by the Spirit, and which the Spirit

did not always allow him to carry out (adapted from R. L. Whiteside, *Commentary on Romans* [Denton, TX: Inys Whiteside, 1945]), 14.

20 James Burton Coffman, *Commentary on Romans* (Austin, TX: Firm Foundation, 1973), 20. "Several conjectures about the origin of the Roman church have been made. It may have arisen through converts among the visitors from Rome, both Jews and proselytes, who were present at Pentecost (Acts 2:10). The close connection between the Jews of Palestine and those of Rome has also been suggested as the historic root from which the church grew. A third suggestion is that the church at Rome may have been the result of a missionary thrust by the Hellenistic Christians at Antioch" (H. Lietzmann, *Beginnings of the Christian Church* [Eng. tr. 1937], pp. 144f.). A more widely held view (and, to this writer, the most probable) is that the church at Rome had its origin in the mixed multitude of travelers to Rome (officials, civil servants, soldiers, merchants) who brought the gospel with them from the East" (Miller, "Romans," *ISBE* [electronic]).

21 "I am not ashamed" is a literary device called a litotes: a negative expression of a positive statement. In other words, Paul is saying: "I am very proud of the gospel" (R. C. H. Lenski, *The Interpretation of St. Paul's Epistle to the Romans* [Peabody, MS: Hendrickson Publishers, 1998], 71.

22 "Power" is from *dunamis*, the Greek word from which we get "dynamic" and "dynamite" (A. T. Robertson, Word Pictures in the New Testament, electronic edition [© 1932, 1960, by the Sunday School Board of the Southern Baptist Convention; database © 2007 by WORDsearch Corp.], on 1:16). However, there is no definite article ("the") in the original Greek; it is simply, "power of God" (Whiteside, *Commentary*, 16).

23 C. K. Barrett, The Epistle to the Romans (New York: Harper & Row, 1957), 30.

24 Lenski, for one, argues that making 1:18–32 refer to "Gentiles" is incorrect; "Paul is speaking of 'men,' the word "Gentiles" [in the Greek] does not appear" (*Interpretation*, 94; bracketed words are mine). Technically, this is true: Paul is addressing all people, not only non-Jews. Yet the context clearly focuses the sinful behaviors of the ancient heathens and pagans much more than it does the ancient Israelites. Also, the fact that Paul speaks directly to Jews in 2:17–29 would create an unnecessary and awkward redundancy, as if to read: "You Jews are guilty; but let me tell you again that you are guilty." This present study maintains that Paul speaks to both groups separately.

25 Lipscomb argues that the ancient Gentiles did not have specific knowledge of God's will regarding their salvation, citing Eph. 2:12 and 1 Cor. 1:21 (*Romans*, 34–35). While this is true, it is not Paul's point. These ancients did not turn away from a codified plan of salvation; they turned away from God Himself. If they had not done this, then they would have sought God through those who did know Him (such as Noah, Melchizedek, Job, Jethro, etc.).

26 Lard, *Commentary*, 49.

27 Lenski, *Interpretation*, 92.

28 Coffman, *Commentary*, 39.

29 By "morality" (or righteousness), we understand this to mean a general sense of right and wrong or good and evil. Although not all people know of God's specific laws (e.g., the Ten Commandments or the gospel of Christ), Paul implies that all people are born with a sense of moral responsibility to a Higher Power (God) and a sense of human decency that is dictated by this Power.

30 Lipscomb paraphrases: "They imagined themselves wise enough to live without God" (*Romans*, 37).

31 We should note here also that ingratitude (the refusal to give thanks) and irreverence (turning away from God) go together: if one exists, so does the other. (The opposite is also true: genuine gratitude toward God will always manifest itself in genuine reverence for Him and vice versa.)

32 Robertson, *Word Pictures* (electronic), on 1:22; bracketed words are mine.

33 Whiteside, *Commentary*, 35.

34 On this point, we cannot ignore God's unmistakable judgment against Sodom and Gomorrah for this very thing (Gen. 19). In 2 Peter 2:7, such people are "unprincipled"—i.e., those who have no respect for law or authority; in Jude 1:7, they are described as having "indulged in gross immorality." Despite its growing acceptance and alleged normalcy today, the entire Bible explicitly and consistently condemns homosexual behavior.

35 The "wrath of God"—His settled, righteous anger—is against all such unrighteousness, and "comes upon the sons of disobedience" (Eph. 5:6). While today it is popular (and convenient) either to minimize this wrath or dismiss it altogether, the gospel is clear and consistent concerning God's burning anger toward those who purposely and defiantly abandon His divine nature.

36   Barrett, *The Epistle to the Romans*, 38.
37   "God did not cause their impurity, but He abandoned them to the natural consequences of the lusts already working in them" (Lipscomb, *Romans*, 39).
38   Strong, *Dictionary* (electronic), G93.
39   *Ibid.*, G4189.
40   "It is scarcely necessary to show that this [i.e., murder] was common among the Gentiles. It has prevailed in all communities, but it was particularly prevalent in Rome. It is necessary only to refer the reader to the common events in the Roman history of assassinations, deaths by poison, and the destruction of slaves. But in a special manner the charge was properly alleged against them, on account of the inhuman contests of the gladiators in the amphitheaters. These were common at Rome, and constituted a favorite amusement with the people. Originally, captives, slaves, and criminals were trained up for combat; but it afterwards became common for even Roman citizens to engage in these bloody combats; and Nero at one show exhibited no less than four hundred senators and six hundred knights as gladiators" (Albert Barnes, *Barnes' Notes on the New Testament,* electronic edition, [database © by WORDsearch Corp.], on 1:29; bracketed words are mine).
41   Strong, *Dictionary* (electronic), G1388.
42   Marvin R. Vincent, *Word Studies in the New Testament,* vol. 3, electronic edition (database © 2014 by WORDsearch Corp.), on 1:29.
43   Robertson, *Word Pictures* (electronic), on 1:29.
44   Barnes, *Notes* (electronic), on 1:29.
45   Robertson, *Word Pictures* (electronic), on 1:30.
46   Vincent, *Word Studies* (electronic), on 1:30.
47   Strong, *Dictionary* (electronic), G794.
48   Barnes, *Notes* (electronic), on 1:31.
49   Whiteside, *Commentary*, 47.
50   Concerning "the darkness"—what it is, how it is so seductive, and why it is so powerful—I strongly recommend my book, *This World Is Not Your Home* (Spiritbuilding Publishers, 2022); go to www.spiritbuilding.com/chad.
51   The "you" in 2:4–5 is used editorially, not accusatorily. Paul is not saying, "You Roman Christians are doing what I am describing," but rather, "Anyone is capable of what I am describing, and those who do so will

receive a corresponding punishment." On 2:5, Luther says, "From this we learn what a hardened heart really is, namely, a heart that despises God's goodness, forbearance, long-suffering. It receives innumerable blessings and yet it commits countless sins and never thinks of mending its evil ways" (Commentary, 54).

52 The phrase, "without the Law" (2:12), does not imply the complete absence of any law but a law different than that which governed the Jews; see similar expressions in 1 Cor. 9:19–21. In most cases in Romans, the definite article ("the") is not in the original Greek text. Thus, the capitalization of "Law" is at the discretion of the translators, since in the Greek text all letters are capitalized. A more accurate rendering of "the Law" would be "law"; yet in some cases, the context does imply the Law of Moses, or simply, "the Law."

53 "The construction of the Greek shows plainly that it was the work of the law, and not the law itself, that was written on the hearts of the Gentiles. This, of course, referred to the moral requirements of the law" (Whiteside, Commentary, 58).

54 Jim McGuiggan, The Book of Romans (Lubbock, TX: Montex Publishing Co., 1982), 103.

55 Commenting on 2:12, Robertson says: "This is a very important statement. The heathen who sin are lost, because they do not keep the law which they have, not because they do not have the Mosaic Law or Christianity" (Word Pictures [electronic]). Lard remarks: "This [2:12] would seem to teach that all, without exception, who have so sinned, will be lost. But such is not the case. The meaning is, that all who have so sinned, and are lost, will be lost without law [to justify or save them]" (Commentary, 83, bracketed words are mine).

56 "Covenant" and "law" are not the same things, even though they are very closely related. Covenant defines the terms by which two or more parties can function as they mutually work toward a stated goal. Law—for those under covenant—describes the expected behavior or appropriate responses of those who are bound by covenant.

57 "My gospel" does not mean Paul owned the gospel of Christ any more than he owned God when he said "my God" (recall 1:8). He only means here "the gospel that I preach," as in 1 Cor. 15:1–2.

58 In fact, God sought from the Jews a circumcision of their hearts, not mere physical circumcision; see Deut. 10:16, Jer. 4:4, Acts 7:51, etc.

59   See Gal. 6:12–15 and Phil. 3:2–3. See also Rev. 2:9, where Jesus refers to "those who say they are Jews but are not, but are a synagogue of Satan"—i.e., those who claimed to be in spiritual fellowship with God, yet their actions forced a different conclusion.

60   This point does not invalidate or render unnecessary circumcision, if indeed that is what God commanded. The emphasis here is on priority, not exclusivity. First, God says, in essence, "Get your heart right and thus put your faith in Me," for the one whose genuine faith is in God will certainly honor whatever else God has called him to do.

61   Ironically, this is the core position of Calvinism (a.k.a. "Doctrine of Predestination"): God saves or condemns whomever He chooses before and regardless of the choices each person makes (see "Appendix").

62   McGuiggan, The Book of Romans, 117; my paraphrase.

63   Lard, Commentary, 104.

64   These quotes are from (in the order used): Psalm 14:1–3, 53:1–3, 5:9, 140:3, 10:7, Prov. 1:16, 1:15–16, Isa. 59:7–8, and Psalm 36:1. While Paul quotes (sometimes loosely) from the Septuagint—the Greek translation of the Hebrew OT (ca. 200 BC)—his own renderings of these passages are as authoritative as the ones from which they came.

65   "Since in the preceding series of quotations the apostle has never quoted from the Decalogue [Ten Commandments] or even, in general, from the Pentateuch, but only from the Psalms, Prophets, and [Holy] Writings, it is clear that the term "the law" must refer to the Old Testament as a whole" (William Hendriksen, The New Testament Commentary: Exposition of Paul's Epistle to the Romans [Grand Rapids: Baker Book House, 1981], 124; bracketed words are mine).

66   While the Scriptures teach that people cannot be justified by law (because every person sins against God's law), Jesus is an exception: He is the only Man in all history who literally was justified by law. It is His perfect obedience to law that makes Him worthy to be our atoning sacrifice, the Source of our salvation (Heb. 5:7–9). Yet, Paul's point is that even though God's law condemns the lawbreaker, it cannot rectify his problem. Law can reveal the solution—and it always does—but it cannot impart the solution.

67   Strong, Dictionary (electronic), G5420.

68   Barnes, Notes (electronic), on 3:19.

69   Recall from "Introduction" of this workbook, "righteousness" and "justification" are related but not equal. "Righteousness" refers to being

godly in one's conduct; it is a state of being which God confers upon a person who imitates His holy behavior. "Justification" is a legal term, which refers to one's innocence before God, the price for his innocence having been sufficiently satisfied by another (Christ). Both terms necessarily imply forgiveness, for one can be neither righteous nor justified otherwise (adapted from Barrett, The Epistle to the Romans, 75–76).

70   "Fall short" is an ever-present, infinitive, continuous phrase: each person continues to sin against God's holiness even after having done it once. Having sinned against law, we thereafter continue to fall short of being justified by that law. Jesus Christ is the only exception to this; having kept the Law of Moses perfectly, He has therefore completed (fulfilled) the Law (Mat. 5:17).

71   "Propitiation" [Greek, hilasterion] is translated "mercy seat" in Heb. 9:5. "Mercy seat" refers to the lid of the ark of the covenant; once a year it was sprinkled with blood on the Day of Atonement (Lev. 16). The fact that we are sprinkled with Jesus' blood (1 Peter 1:2) leads us to conclude that He has become to us the living substance of what the ancient mercy seat was to Israel: the union of earthly blood and divine mercy, which provides atonement for sins. But Coffman rightfully adds: "There must certainly far more in the meaning of this word than men can fully comprehend in this life" (Commentary, 133).

72   The traditional idea of God "rolling forward" His forgiveness of faithful people who lived prior to Christ's sacrifice is unbiblical. God did not "roll forward" His forgiveness; He forgave those people upon their having demonstrated faith in Him (through obedience to whatever He required of them). The numerous passages in Leviticus, for example, in which the Israelite was forgiven (4:20, 26, 31, 5:10, 13, etc.), and David's own words (Psalm 32:1, 51:1–2, etc.), do not indicate a postponed forgiveness but a full and complete one. In other words, God was so confident that His Son would be the perfect sacrifice for sin, He forgave people in full even before Christ's blood for that forgiveness had not yet been shed (on His cross).

73   By this, I mean: if you remove one's blood from his body, his earthly life ceases to be. Just as the body without the spirit is dead (James 2:26), so the body without blood is dead. Blood symbolizes the essence of one's spiritual life (or consciousness) in the earthly context.

74   "The act, therefore, which the sinner is required to perform, in order to be made a partaker of the righteousness of God, is to believe on Christ; that

is, to receive him as he is revealed in the gospel as the eternal Son of God…" (Hodge, Commentary, 89; emphasis is mine).

75   Literally, "apart from law"—there is no definite article here in the Greek text (Whiteside, Commentary, 75).

76   "Here we may draw hurtful conclusions, if we do not keep in mind Paul's line of argument. Paul is not contrasting faith and the obedience of faith [to law—MY WORDS], but he is contrasting justification by works of law and justification by faith. …Works of law is an entirely different thing from obedience of faith" (Whiteside, 83). Understanding this will avoid the error of Origen and Martin Luther (and others), which is to add the word "only" to the text after "justified by faith" (Barrett, The Epistle to the Romans, 82). We are justified by faith; yet this faith must be demonstrated by obedience to works of law. "Faith only" or "faith alone" [Latin, sola fide] (see Hodge, Commentary, 100) implies that no works of obedience are required before God will pronounce a man justified—which contradicts Paul's argument in chapter 4. "Apart from works of law" only implies an act of God; it does not mean "apart from the need for human obedience" (recall 1:5, "the obedience of faith").

77   "One of the strangest things in all the field of Bible exegesis is the contention so generally made that this language [in Gen. 15:6] refers to the justification of Abraham as an alien sinner" (Whiteside, Commentary, 89). I am not convinced this is among the strangest things, but his point here is that Abraham had already proved his faith in God, and God had already expressed His favor with Abraham (Gen. 15:1). The statement that "Abraham believed" was not a sudden epiphany, as though he had not believed up to that point. Rather, he proved himself to be a believer, and God credited him with righteousness based upon that proof.

78   Once again, it cannot be argued that David's sins were "rolled forward," as some assume. David himself says that his sins were "forgiven," "covered [lit., atoned for]," and not "taken into account."

79   We might also consider here Job, who was likely a contemporary of Abraham. Yet, in Job's case there is no mention of any written law, circumcision, or specific priesthood. Even so, God forgave Job and (because of Job's intercession) his three friends based upon blood sacrifices and their repentance—i.e., their acts of faith.

80   "To believe in hope is to believe in connection with it, or to have hope to accompany the belief. Abraham believed all God said, and hoped for all

He promised. Belief is the basis of hope; hence where there is no belief, there is no hope" (Lard, Commentary, 146).

81 "Standing" before God as justified people is deliberately set in contrast against the "fallen" nature of the sinful, unconverted heart (3:23). To "stand" in this context often means "to find favor with [God]" and is synonymous with salvation (as in 1 Cor. 15:1 and Jude 1:24).

82 Many commentators wrangle over the exact translation of the Greek: "we have peace" versus "let us have peace" (and so with "we stand" versus "let us stand"; "we exult" versus "let us exult"). "Let us have" is too passive here; it suggests that we experience such peace only when we consciously think about it. The context, if nothing else, should determine the answer: justification by faith does indeed produce peace, whether one consciously experiences it (Phil. 4:7). The peace is spiritual, not only emotional; however, it is not optional—not for one who desired to be justified by God. "Peace is a fact which results from justification, not something which the justified are merely exhorted to have, but may not have" (Lard, Commentary, 153).

83 If one wishes to understand "God" to be Jesus Christ, there is no contradiction with this, since Jesus is God. As the Son of God who has proved Himself worthy (Rev. 5:11–13), Christ certainly is able to justify human souls.

84 "This peace consists properly in an appeased conscience and in confidence in God, just as conversely the lack of peace means spiritual anxiety, a disturbed conscience and mistrust over [and] against God" (Luther, Commentary, 89; bracketed word is mine).

85 "Tribulations" refers to "pressures," but means troubles, persecutions, or burdens (Strong, Dictionary [electronic], G2347); see John 16:33 and Acts 14:22.

86 Lenski, Interpretation, 338.

87 "The language [of 5:6] does not mean that we are now unable to believe God nor do what He commands [which is Calvinistic]. It refers to man's helplessness without the death of Christ. Men were condemned sinners, with no means of escape from sin and condemnation. They were helpless. But the death of Christ opened up the way of escape, and removed the weakness spoken of in this verse" (Whiteside, Commentary, 117; bracketed words are mine).

88 I have written on this subject in my book, This World Is Not Your Home

(Spiritbuilding Publishers, 2022); go to www.spiritbuilding.com/chad.

89   "Reconciliation" is from a Latin base (reconcilio), but the Greek word Paul uses here is katallasso, "to change mutually; to compound a difference" (Strong, Dictionary [electronic], G2644). "The verb means primarily to exchange; and hence to change the relation of hostile parties into a relation of peace; to reconcile" (Vincent, Word Studies [electronic], on 5:10).

90   Moses Lard notes that we are reconciled to God, not the other way around: God does not change, but we are most certainly changed by Him. We once were disobedient and enemies; now we in Christ are obedient and friends of God (Commentary, 159).

91   The Doctrine of Original Sin, which has been incorporated into Calvinism, claims that all people are born guilty of Adam's sin—the "original sin"—and therefore are condemned by God upon birth. This assumes that we are all inherently corrupted and have a sinful nature (a.k.a. "total hereditary depravity") and is the basis for baptizing babies and young children (see "Appendix").

92   Hodge makes an intriguing point: "Sin existed before the fall of Adam. … Sin entered the world; it invaded the race. There is a personification of sin, as afterwards of death. Both are represented as hostile and evil powers, which obtained dominion over main" (Commentary, 146). I have reached the same conclusion in my book, This World Is Not Your Home (Spiritbuilding Publishers, 2022); go to www.spiritbuilding.com/chad.

93   Lard, Commentary, 167. "Accordingly, though we all suffer for Adam's sin, no one of us will ever be judged for it. For our sins only will we be judged" (169).

94   The point here has to do with when a person becomes a sinner: is it when he is born (as Calvinism teaches; see Hodge, Commentary, 149), or is it when he commits sin (as Scripture teaches)? If it is when he is born, then he is born guilty, even though he has not yet sinned; if it is when he sins, then each person is responsible for his own sin and does not bear the guilt of someone else's sin. Likewise, the "when" question bears upon one's redemption: when does one become redeemed by Christ? Is it when Christ died (regardless of our faith in Him), or is it because He died and when we put our faith in Him? Even though Christ's death brings justification to "all men" (5:18), one is not born of God (John 1:12) simply because Christ died but only when he puts his faith in Christ's death (and all that it involves). Hodge, following others, says that "because all sinned" means "all

are constituted as sinners," meaning, all are regarded and treated as sinners (ibid., 154), but this is not what Paul said here and twists his words to fit a predetermined doctrine.

95 The idea that we all have a "sinful nature," and that this is what causes us to sin, misrepresents the reality of our situation. Our "nature" is not determined by Adam or sin but by our own personal choices to succumb, eventually, to our own lustful desires rather than to honor the moral code that God has built into our conscience (James 1:13–16; recall comments on 2:12–16). Some say, "We are sinners because we are the sons of a sinner. A sinner can beget only a sinner, who is like him" (Luther, Commentary, 95). But this confuses the father's guilt for his own sin and the effect of that guilt upon his posterity, versus the communication or transmission of such guilt. This also would require that Jesus was "a sinner," since He was born as a Man into humanity—a blasphemous idea. Even the Law of Moses says a man can be perfectly sinless—and justified by law—if he keeps the Law perfectly (Lev. 18:5; see Gal. 3:12). A perfectly law-abiding man cannot be born sinful and at the same time justified by law.

96 The physical curse remains for as long as we are bound to a physical system. Even though Christ has saved our souls, our bodies are still destined to die—the result of the curse upon Adam and his posterity. But we are promised that, once we are in God's world, we will never die but will have eternal life (John 11:25–26, 1 John 2:25).

97 Barrett agrees: "[The two] do not correspond as exact equivalents. The act of grace does not balance the act of sin; it overbalances it" (The Epistle to the Romans, 113).

98 Paul does not say that every person is automatically guilty of Adam's sin, any more than he says that every person is automatically saved by Christ's righteousness. He is drawing a contrast between the two men and their actions, not removing our personal responsibility or accountability to God for our actions.

99 Luther, Commentary, 98; bracketed words are mine.

100 "Baptism" [Greek, baptizo] means "to be whelmed (fully wet)"; immersion (in water) (Strong, Dictionary [electronic], G907). For a full study on "baptism," I recommend my book, Being Born of God: The Role and Significance of Baptism in Becoming a Christian (Spiritbuilding Publishers, 2014); go to www.spiritbuilding.com/chad.

101 Kenneth Wuest has some excellent comments on this ("Romans," Word

Studies in the Greek New Testament [Grand Rapids: Eerdmans Publishing Co., 1955; reprinted, 1992], 92–98).

102 "Baptism 'into Christ Jesus' betokens incorporation into Him, so that henceforth the baptized person is 'in Christ Jesus'; sharing Christ's death he has died to the old way, and sharing His resurrection he lives in the new way. To live in sin would be, for such a person, a contradiction of his life in Christ; it would be repudiating his baptism, severing himself from Christ" (Bruce, "Romans," Zondervan, 156).

103 In the same way, both circumcision and the Sabbath were signs of the covenant between God and Israel. Yet, God required these signs to be observed. Failure to keep the "sign of the covenant" indicated a disregard for the laws that commanded such observances, and the God who gave such laws (Gen. 17:14, Ezek. 20:19–21). This principle also applies to baptism: even though it serves as a sign of our covenant with God (Col. 2:9–12), it is also a command of God to those who wish to call upon His name (Acts 2:38, 10:48, and 22:16).

104 For example, Teacher Bible Commentary says, "Thus baptism is a dynamic symbol which has meaning for the new Christian. It helps to strengthen his determination to live a new life. It is not essential to salvation: it is essential to a full Christian life" (H. Franklin Paschall and Hershel H. Hobbs, eds., electronic edition [© 1972 by Broadman Press; database © 2009 by WORDsearch Corp.], on Rom. 6:1 – 7:6). This is just a bunch of words without meaning. As many commentators say of baptism, in so many words, "It is not essential, but it is important." This begs the question: why would God give us important instructions that are not essential? Who decided that this action is important but not essential? It was certainly not Paul.

105 We must say "believer" here and not "Christian" because the one pursuing baptism is not yet a Christian. It is baptism that defines one as a Christian once the other requirements of conversion have been met. Christians are not baptized; one cannot "walk in newness of life" without being baptized. (One can choose to believe he has this "newness of life" apart from baptism, but that will not change his spiritual relationship with God.) To be "born again" of God, one must obey God's instructions (Mat. 28:19); being born again is not something one says but is something one does in faith.

106 Water is a most appropriate element for the "born again" process: the

earth was "born" out of water and was re-born through water (2 Peter 3:5–6), and every human is born out of the "water" of the womb. Water, then, serves as a consistent symbol of birth and re-birth. While God performs His work upon the human soul during conversion, the believer performs his work (of faith) in water; thus, one is "born again" both in an earthly and spiritual context—that is, "of water and the Spirit" (John 3:5). In a very real sense, we are saved through water—not by water, but not without it, either. Water is merely a physical element; baptism in water is an act of faith. The emphasis is on the action in water, and not water alone (thus, 1 Peter 3:21).

107 "It is altogether probable that the apostle in this place had allusion to the custom of baptizing by immersion" (Barnes, *Notes* [electronic], on 6:4). One wonders: what else could Paul have meant? And what is baptism but "immersion"—for this is exactly the meaning of the word? "It is a tragedy that Paul's majestic picture here has been so blurred by controversy [or sheer disbelief] that some refuse to see it. It should be said also that a symbol [i.e., baptism] is not the reality, but the picture of the reality" (Robertson, *Word Pictures* [electronic], 362; bracketed words are mine).

108 Regarding 6:7, Lenski writes concerning Christians, "Paul is not speaking of our guilt of sin but of sin's power to make us sin" (Interpretation, 403). But a Christian, though he once "died to sin," can be guilty of sin when he commits it. Sin cannot "make" us do anything without our consent, whether that consent was given up front (in the case of addictions) or on each occasion of temptation. The responsibility to sin does not lie with sin itself, however powerful the temptation might be, but with each person who commits it.

109 "Our death depends so entirely on Christ's sacrificial death by crucifixion that, when he is stressing this connection, Paul is able to say that baptism nails our old man of sin on Christ's cross in order to perish in and with the sins for which Christ died on his cross" (Lenski, *Interpretation*, 401). This forces one to consider the magnitude of our having died with Christ—as if on the same cross (Gal. 2:20).

110 This also refutes the popular doctrine of Premillennialism, which necessarily implies that Jesus must come back to earth and reign for 1,000 years in Jerusalem to finish what He left undone. Such doctrines contradict the "once for all" work of Jesus Christ, and insinuate that Christ failed to do all the work He was sent to do (John 17:4). This also begs the awful question: If Jesus failed the first time, what assurance do we have that He will

not fail again?

111 Something to consider: "Although it is the body in focus here, the mind is also an 'instrument' no less than members of the body; and all such instruments are used at the direction and according to the will of the true person, which, in the Christian, is the seat of the inner reign of Christ in human hearts" (Coffman, *Commentary*, 236). Whiteside adds: "Certainly the body, being merely an instrument, is not responsible for the sin [of a man]; and if the spirit of the regenerate [i.e., convert] is not responsible for the sin, it would seem that a regenerate man is not in any sense responsible for the wrong that he does!" (*Commentary*, 137, bracketed words are mine).

112 For a much fuller study on this subject, I strongly recommend by book, *The New Testament Pattern: God's Plan for Christians and Their Churches* (Spiritbuilding Publishing, 2023); go to www.spiritbuilding.com/chad.

113 It is not necessary here for Paul to expound upon any exceptions to this, as in the case of immorality (Mat. 19:9) or abandonment (1 Cor. 7:15). His purpose is only to discuss the effect that physical death has on an earth-bound relationship. His case in point is marriage, but his primary explanation has to do with one's severance from sin (through having died to it) to become legally bound to Christ. "The case of the wife and the husband is adduced, not as a figure, but merely as an illustration. The translation therefore should express the fact simply, and not conform to a supposed figure" (Lard, *Commentary*, 224).

114 Lard thinks that "Spirit" here should be in lower-case: "The word spirit here denotes, not the Holy Spirit, but the human, the spirit of the disciple" (Commentary, 227). Yet Paul uses nearly the exact same language in 2 Cor. 3:2–18 in reference to the Holy Spirit. All said, "newness of the Spirit" has a virtual dual-meaning in this context: the Holy Spirit is the source of renewal (Titus 3:4–7), but the human spirit enjoys the effects and benefits of this renewal.

115 Divine grace operates outside the realm of written law. Law can define grace, lead us to it, and encourage us to seek it, but it cannot offer it. Grace does what law (or imperfect law-keeping) cannot do. On the other hand, law and grace work hand-in-hand: grace is irrelevant if there is no law, because then there is no sin to atone for (Rom. 4:15); law's condemnation cannot be overcome if there is no grace by which to escape it. Thus, we do not choose between law and grace, but we accept them both in their proper contexts.

116 "It is not surprising that it was especially this tenth commandment

that stopped Paul in his tracks. The other commandments, superficially interpreted, forbid transgressions that are, or seem to be, of a more or less external character. ... But the tenth commandment strikes directly at the very root of sin, namely, man's sinful heart, his evil desire" (Hendriksen, *NTC*, 220).

117 We should remember that Jesus was condemned because He allegedly blasphemed against the Law (Mat. 26:63–66). Likewise, Stephen was accused of speaking against the Law (Acts 6:11–14)—and Paul painfully remembered his part in consenting to Stephen's execution (Acts 7:58). These two incidents no doubt motivate Paul to respond vigorously to any charge that he was trying to undermine the Law (Acts 24:14–15).

118 "There are some ... who denied that the Apostle here speaks of his own person, and indeed of himself as being spiritual and not carnal. But the whole passage shows very clearly a strong hatred against the flesh and a sincere love for the Law and all that is good. No carnal man ever does this" (Luther, *Commentary*, 112).

119 Barrett, *The Epistle to the Romans*, 147.

120 *Ibid.*, 149.

121 Lard, *Commentary*, 247.

122 For an in-depth study of the Spirit and His work, I recommend my book, *The Holy Spirit of God: A Biblical Perspective* (Spiritbuilding Publishers, 2010); go to www.spiritbuilding.com/chad.

123 This "likeness" calls to mind the bronze serpent incident in Num. 21:6–9. The Israelites, because of their sinning against God, were bitten by serpents; God told Moses to put a likeness of the serpent—in reality, a likeness of the affliction—upon a pole, so that those bitten could look upon the bronze serpent and be healed. This is a "type" prophecy of what Christ did, which He Himself cited (John 3:14–15). The serpent(s) did not literally become bronzed any more than Jesus literally became a sinner; in both cases, a representative figure was used.

124 While Jesus died for us, God did not punish Him for us. The animals sacrificed to God under the Law of Moses were not being punished; they were slain as a representative of the one for whom they died. So it is with Christ: men punished Him for His alleged crimes, but God found Him completely innocent. An innocent man is not deserving of punishment, and God never punishes innocent people.

125 "Many persons in the first century world felt that an unalterable hostility

existed between matter and spirit (thought or consciousness) with matter being the source of evil and spirit being the fountain of good. Paul made use of this kind of language but not with the dualism of Greek thought which opposed flesh (matter) to spirit. Flesh, as substance or material, is in itself neutral and has neither evil or good nature; but a person under sin's control is 'in the flesh' (8:9), a contrast to life 'in the Spirit' (8:9–11). In this life (in the flesh) believers must rise to the demand of God's gift to us through Christ and walk 'according to the Spirit' (8:4–8)" (Songer, "Romans," Holman Bible Dictionary [electronic]).

126 This is true generally as well as specifically. Generally, the Spirit gives life to all creatures: just as God breathed life into Adam (Gen. 2:7), so He "breathes" life into all things, for nothing can exist apart from Him. Specifically, the Spirit gives "life" (i.e., fellowship with God) to the soul of the believer since the believer has access to the Father because of the Spirit (Eph. 2:18). The Holy Spirit is God: wherever the Spirit is, God is. Christ, in His unique position as man's Redeemer, stands between sinful man and holy God and reconciles the two through Himself (Col. 1:19–21), making the indwelling of the Spirit possible.

127 See also 2 Cor. 3:17 and 1 Peter 1:10–12, where the same interchangeable usage also occurs.

128 In a parallel (but not exact) scenario, Paul describes Timothy as a "kindred spirit" who knows Paul's heart better than anyone else (Phil. 2:20–22). It might be said, then, that Paul's spirit and Timothy's spirit were united on one purpose and given over to the same work, which is what Paul is saying about the Holy Spirit being both "of God" and "of Christ" all at once.

129 Barrett, *The Epistle to the Romans*, 158.

130 The subject of bodily resurrection is a difficult one for many Christians. This is largely because of what Paul says in 1 Cor. 15:40–49, which seems at first to contradict the idea that we will be raised from the grave with our identifiable earthly bodies. But it is very likely that Paul is speaking of different stages of the same event in both passages. Jesus' literal, physical body was raised from the dead; it cannot be otherwise. His resurrected body manifested certain properties that it did not have before, but it was still Jesus' body. However, He did not remain in that body as He ascended from earth since "flesh and blood" have no place in the spiritual realm of God (1 Cor. 15:50). At some point, His body was transformed into something different than a physical body (Phil. 3:20–21). There is no reason to believe it will

be different for us: Jesus will call us forth from the grave (John 5:25–29, 1 Thess. 4:16) and, like those who are alive at His coming (1 Cor. 15:51–52), "we will be changed" as we enter glory.

131 Lenski, *Interpretation*, 517.

132 Gender is irrelevant here. The reason for the "son" designation has to do with a right to an inheritance rather than a male or female distinction.

133 The unnaturalness of our sonship to God is evident in the fact that we are "born again" (John 3:3, 1 Peter 1:3). It is natural to be born once; to be "born again" is entirely unnatural and defies every expectation of life as we know it in the physical universe. Thus, we are made sons only through a supernatural process—one which transcends every natural process—and yet this adoption still guarantees that we will be heirs of God.

134 "The reference here is a Roman legal process by which one man took another's to be his own son. The adopted son took the name and rank of the one adopting him and stood in exactly the same legal relation to him as a born son" (J. W. Shepherd, in Lipscomb, *Romans*, 150).

135 Lexicographers and commentators are nearly split on whether the word here should be "creation" or "creature." Lenski chooses to replace "creation" in this passage with "creature world" (*Interpretation*, 534).

136 The following points are cited in Hendriksen, *NTC*, 266; a similar list is found in Lard, *Commentary*, 269.

137 To our knowledge, angels either live in God's presence, or live in an irretrievably condemned state of being; there is no intermediate existence or expectation of salvation (Heb. 2:16).

138 Vincent, *Word Studies* (electronic), on 8:20.

139 See also Heb. 2:6–8, where the writer shows that "all things" (of God's Creation) have been put in subjection to man. But when the ruler has been corrupted, this negatively affects all that he rules, which is that to which Paul refers here in 8:19–20. "As a result of Adam's sin, the whole creation was cursed and fell away from its original design and became subject to the reign of death" (Lipscomb, *Romans*, 153).

140 This does not mean—and does not have to mean—that God will restore the physical world to its original paradise-like state. Such is the teaching of Premillennialists and other literalists and semi-literalists who believe that God's intention is to restore the earth so that humans can live here forever, as in the beginning. But God has made it clear that the redeemed will live in God's world (John 14:1–3, Phil. 1:23, 1 Thess. 4:17,

etc.). Furthermore, the physical creation will "pass away" (Mat. 24:35, 2 Peter 3:10–12, 1 John 2:15–17, etc.), as it is corrupted with sin and must be destroyed. Jesus did not die to save the physical creation but human souls. The souls of the redeemed will be the only remnant of this physical life that will enter heavenly glory.

141 Lenski, *Interpretation*, 536.

142 This phrase ("having the first fruits of the Spirit") may refer to miraculous gifts of the Spirit or the indwelling of the Spirit. This latter definition seems the most practical, in lieu of any further definition; it is also consistent with other NT passages (Gal. 5:22–23, Eph. 5:9, and Phil. 1:11). However, Whiteside makes a good argument for the miraculous gifts of the Spirit as being His "first fruits" (*Commentary*, 184). Regardless, this is an admittedly difficult passage to fully understand.

143 "[Christians'] redemption in Christ will not be completed until their bodies are raised from the dead and glorified and are become like Jesus in His glorified and immortal state" (Lipscomb, *Romans*, 155). While Paul does not mention bodily resurrection here, this does seem to be the underlying thought.

144 "It is uncertain whether Paul means unspoken or unspeakable groans" (Barrett, *The Epistle to the Romans*, 168; emphasis his). Admittedly, we are denied a fuller explanation on this than what is provided here.

145 Robertson, *Word Pictures* (electronic), on 8:26; Wuest, *Word Studies*, 140.

146 Being "called" necessarily implies that an invitation has been offered and (in this case) a response was made. God calls us through His gospel (1 Cor. 1:9, 2 Thess. 2:13–14, and 1 Peter 2:9); we call upon God through our response to it (compare Acts 2:21 and 2:39). This response must be accompanied by proper demonstrations of obedience (Acts 22:16, Rom. 10:9–13, etc.). "[T]hose who love the Lord" necessarily implies decisions made not by God but by all those who have believed in Christ.

147 Calvinism teaches that each person (lit., every single soul) is predestined by God to be saved or condemned; the decision has already been determined before we are born. Luther says that those who are elect cannot be lost, and those who are not elect (the "reprobate") cannot be saved. Yet, the lost are supposed to glory in the fact that God's will is being done (*Commentary*, 132). Naturally, Luther (as do all Calvinists) sees himself as one of the "elect," and therefore speaks almost glibly about the

"reprobate." Yet Paul is consistent in his usage of "predestined": it is always in reference to Christ's church, not to the individual Christian (as in Eph. 1:5, 11).

148 Wuest, *Word Studies,* 145; bracketed word is mine.

149 In this passage, Paul states four great truths concerning Christ: He died (purposely and sacrificially); He was raised from the dead; He is now at the right hand of God; and He now intercedes for us. These four facts form the concrete basis for the Christian faith; without them, we have no gospel and no hope for the future.

150 "Not just: we shall conquer in the end; no, even now we are super-conquerors. And this not—let it be added immediately—by reason of our marvelous character and unflinching courage" (Hendriksen, *NTC,* 292).

151 The proportion compares to the small number of Jews who returned to Judea from Babylonian exile by the decree of Cyrus (2 Chron. 36:20–23). Consider the gospel a kind of heavenly "decree" of far greater value and significance, yet most Jews snubbed God's invitation into His kingdom. In His parables, Jesus expresses His own disappointment in His people (Mat. 21:33–43, 22:1–8, and Luke 14:16–24).

152 This calls to mind Judah's offer to Joseph (Gen. 44:33), Moses' offer to God (Exod. 32:32), and David's lament over Absalom (2 Sam. 18:33). "But most of all, it fixes our attention on him who really became his people's Substitute"—that is, Jesus Christ (Hendriksen, *NTC,* 310; emphasis is his).

153 "The idea, therefore, in these places [citing 1 Kings 20:42 and Isa. 34:5] is simply, 'I could be willing to be destroyed, or devoted to death, for the sake of my countrymen.' And the apostle evidently means to say that he would be willing to suffer the bitterest evils, to forego all pleasure, to endure any privation and toil, nay, to offer his life, so that he might be wholly devoted to sufferings, as an offering, if he might be the means of benefiting and saving the nation" (Barnes, *Notes* [electronic], on 9:3). Moses also offered a similar statement (Exod. 32:32). "[I]f it be understood as the language rather of 'strong and indistinct emotions than of definite ideas' [Hodge], expressing passionately how he felt his whole being swallowed up in the salvation of his people, the difficulty [of this passage] will vanish" (Robert Jamieson, A. R. Fausset, and David Brown, *Commentary Critical and Explanatory on the Whole Bible* (1871), electronic edition [database © 2012 by WORDsearch Corp.], on 9:3).

154 In ancient hereditary custom, the first-born son was due a double

portion of the inheritance. Yet on several occasions in Scripture, the younger son secured an inheritance greater than the older son: Jacob, Isaac, Perez, David, Solomon, etc. In each case, divine providence directed these changed outcomes, underscoring God's ability to alter the normal expectations based on human determination. Besides, "Jehovah's language to Rebekah [recall 9:12; see Gen. 25:23] shows plainly that he was speaking of the descendants of Jacob and Esau rather than of them as individuals" (Whiteside, Commentary, 199; bracketed citations are mine).

155 On 9:15, Luther says: "That means: I [God] will give grace, in time and life, to him concerning whom I purposed from eternity to show mercy. On him will I have compassion to forgive his sin in time and life whom I forgave and pardoned from all eternity" (*Commentary*, 139). Hodge naturally concurs (*Commentary*, 310). This supports Calvinism, but not the text. Luther errs by making Paul's words into a declaration of each man's (Jacob and Esau's) spiritual destination, rather than the earthly context to which he (Paul) clearly refers.

156 "To 'love' and 'hate' as God uses the terms means to approve or disapprove, to bless or curse" (Lipscomb, *Romans*, 172).

157 McGuiggan, *The Book of Romans*, 294.

158 "But what must not be forgotten, and what appears distinctly from the whole narrative, is that Pharaoh's hardening was at first his own act. Five times it is said of him that he himself hardened his heart (Exod. 7:13, 14, 22, 8:15, 32, and 9:7), before the time when at last it is said that God hardened his heart (Exod. 9:12); and even after that, as if a remnant of liberty still remained to him, it is said for the last time that he hardened himself (Exod. 9:34–35). Then at length, as if by way of a terrible retribution, God hardened him five times (Exod. 10:1, 20, 27, 11:10, and 14:8)" (Lipscomb, *Romans*, 176).

159 The best interpretation of the OT is by the inspired writers of the NT. In reading the quotes from Hosea we might not have been certain to apply them to Gentiles; but Paul makes it a fact, and because of this we can speak with confidence on the matter. Paul's apostolic interpretation of Scripture is itself Scripture to us.

160 "It is commonly said: 'The intention is good, and the purpose is true, but the means are misused.' The goal which they [the Jews] seek is correct; but the way is wrong by which they endeavor to reach the goal" (Luther, *Commentary*, 146; bracketed words are mine).

161 Lard, *Commentary*, 323.

162 Paul quotes loosely from Deut. 30:11–14, where Moses reminded Israel that God's will was made evident to them through the Law that He had revealed at Mt. Sinai (Deut. 29:29). Israel did not have to go searching for God's instructions; they only had to obey (in faith) what He said. Thus, even in the time of Moses, God's plan of justification by faith was already in full effect. While the Law of Moses could indeed justify a person who kept it perfectly (Lev. 18:5), no Israelite—save Christ Himself—did this. Furthermore, wherever there is justification by faith, there must be divine grace.

163 The quote here is from Joel 2:32, the same as Peter cited in Acts 2:21 with reference to the "pouring out" of the Holy Spirit upon Christ's church. "Whoever" and "no distinction" (in 10:11–13) indicate that salvation has been extended to all people, regardless of ethnicity, genealogy, or gender.

164 Lenski, *Interpretation*, 658.

165 To some, however, this specifies a minister (or missionary) whose vocation it is to preach the gospel. "Three things only, constitute a call to the ministry, namely: 1. That the preacher shall be a genuine Christian, pious in heart and pure in life. 2. That he have the truth; for God never calls men to preach error. 3. That he possess the ability; for Christ never calls the incompetent. He who has these three qualifications owes it to Christ and the human race to preach; he that lacks them should never attempt it" (Lard, *Commentary*, 338).

166 The word "heed" (or "hearken") in 10:16 is from *hupekousan*, which is translated in nearly every other place in the NT as "obey" or "obedient" (Strong, *Dictionary* [electronic], G5219). It is a stronger meaning than merely "not listening" to something; it refers to a deliberate disobedience of that which was heard. See Coffman (*Commentary*, 376–377) for reasons why translators choose "heed" over "obey."

167 "Paul's method in this place, as so frequently throughout the epistle, is that of the diatribe, in which theoretical questions are raised, as if from a hearer, then refuted" (Coffman, *Commentary*, 379).

168 "By this they [the Jews, as a whole] prove that they did not seek God for His sake, but for their own sakes, because they sinfully loved themselves and hypocritically desired their own advantage. Had they really sought God, they would have been glad that others were saved, and would not have been enraged [at the conversion of the Gentiles]" (Luther, *Commentary*, 152;

bracketed words are mine).

169 The basis for one's having been chosen or hardened is not God's own sovereign decision (as Calvinism teaches), but whether one seeks to be justified by (works of) Law or by faith in God (through Christ; recall 10:3–4). Paul's explanation here in chapter 11 cannot be separated from what he has already said concerning "confessing" and "believing" in chapter 10.

170 This began with Abram (later renamed Abraham), whose own family was a faithful remnant of his extended family in Ur and Haran. Through his faithfulness, the promises (Gen. 12:1–3) were kept alive; because of these promises, God acted on behalf of his descendants, the Israelites (Exod. 6:2–8, Deut. 7:7–8).

171 "Rich root" (11:17) is literally "the root of the fatness," i.e., the rich sap of the tree (Lenski, *Interpretation*, 704–705; Robertson, *Word Pictures* [electronic], on 11:17).

172 "Kindness" means goodness, beneficence, or blessing; "severity" is derived from a root word which literally means "to cut off," as lopping a branch off of a tree (Lenski, Interpretation, 709). "The fault of the Jews lay in their boastfulness and self-confidence (2:17ff.); if the Gentiles fall into the same ways, they will share the same fate" (Barrett, *The Epistle to the Romans*, 218).

173 A case in point would be the people of Noah's day in whose hearts was nothing good but evil continually (Gen. 6:5): they were completely hardened and thus not worth saving (from judgment). Another case would be the Canaanites (Gen. 15:16) or the citizens of Sodom and Gomorrah (Gen. 19). A complete hardening would indicate that no faithful remnant remained; otherwise, God would not have pronounced a curse of extermination upon such people. As it is, God did punish Israel, but He never promised to exterminate His people (Isa. 1:9).

174 See Hendriksen, *NTC*, 378; Lenski, *Interpretation*, 720; and Wuest, *Word Studies*, 199.

175 Or "your rational, sacred service," which captures the essence of what is meant (Wuest, *Word Studies*, 206).

176 McGuiggan, *The Book of Romans*, 353.

177 Lard, *Commentary*, 381.

178 In the Greek text, the entire passage of 12:6–18 is a series of imperative statements; Lenski believes each statement should have an exclamation point (Interpretation, 758–777), and this makes sense. Thus, he renders

these verses literally: "The love—not hypocritical! … Rejoice in company with rejoicing ones! Weep with weeping ones!"—and so for the rest of Paul's brief admonitions in this chapter.

179 Lipscomb, *Romans*, 225.

180 Strong, *Dictionary* (electronic), G5381.

181 "When men conceive the idea that they are wise, they are unwilling to look to God for wisdom" (Lipscomb, *Romans*, 229).

182 Barnes, *Notes* (electronic), on 12:17.

183 Robertson, *Word Pictures* (electronic), on 12:21.

184 Lard, *Commentary*, 398.

185 Political revolution is a special case; Paul's comments here address a general position, not special cases. Regarding the American colonist's Revolutionary War against Great Britain (1775 – 1783), I recommend *Rebellion to Tyrants Is Obedience to God: The Role of Christianity in the American Revolution* by Daniel S. Stackhouse Jr., Ph.D. (CreateSpace Independent Publishing, 2016). You may not agree with all that the colonists believed (or did) at that time, but it is worth looking at their situation as they saw it rather than simply from our present view of things.

186 The case of a "conscientious objector" does not nullify the general principle which Christ has laid down. This person morally opposes the payment of any financial support of his government: it is not just that he dislikes paying taxes or opposes what his tax dollars will go toward; it violates his conscience to participate in taxation. This is more a principle-based position than a realistic one, since it may be impossible (in the United States, anyway) to avoid paying any taxes. Furthermore, one must be extremely careful not to confuse the violation of conscience with one's strong personal disapproval of how the government operates, how it spends (or wastes) its revenue, or similar issues.

187 Some have interpreted Paul's statement here to mean that Christians should not be in debt at all (i.e., prohibiting car loans, revolving credit, mortgages, etc.). "What the Apostle appears to prohibit is not, contracting debt, but owing a thing after it is due" (Lard, *Commentary*, 403). Paying what you owe is far different from being forbidden to owe anything. Paul admits that we will owe taxes, customs, fear (respect), and honor. These must be paid; we cannot avoid paying them on the grounds that we belong to Christ and are thus (assumedly) exempt from such payments to unchristian people or secular institutions. We cannot interpret Paul's words in such a way that

imposes upon them a condition that he never meant.

188 When Paul says in 13:8 that one who loves has fulfilled "{the} law," he seems to reference the Law of Moses. But the definite article ("the") is not in the original Greek; Paul thus refers to law in general—i.e., as that which comes from God. Likewise, the citation of specific laws from the Ten Commandments does not force one to consider only the Law of Moses. The cited commandments are moral laws and thus timeless and immutable; such laws are present in all covenant relationships with God. So then, Paul is not talking about fulfilling the Law of Moses—only Christ was capable of that—but speaks of the Christian's responsibility to fulfill His obligation to God through the demonstration of godly love toward all men.

189 Adapted from Barrett, *The Epistle to the Romans*, 251.

190 Whiteside, *Commentary*, 263.

191 Strong, *Dictionary* (electronic), G2970.

192 *Ibid.*, G2845. The Greek word here is *koite*, which means "bed" or "chambering"; it is the word from which we get "coitus," which means sexual intercourse.

193 "The 'strong' brother is not called upon to settle all the scruples of the 'weak' brother. But each takes it on himself to do it" (Robertson, *Word Pictures* [electronic], on 14:1).

194 "Obstacle" (14:13) is from *proskomma*, an offense or stone of stumbling. "Stumbling block" is from *skandalon*, from which we also get "scandalous." That which is offensive to a brother in Christ is scandalous to God: He finds such action shameful and unbecoming of His children. "A stumbling block is always placed and placed for someone else" (Lenski, *Interpretation*, 847); it is not an accident but is a deliberate imposition or an intentional carelessness or unconcern for another's welfare.

195 The key to this passage involves determining what constitutes sin or not. It is not sinful to have a certain personal conviction about what you eat, or what religious day of the year you may honor if these convictions do not conflict with what God has already determined in His gospel. There are two ways to sin against God: direct violation of His word and a violation of one's own conscience. This does not mean that conscience is equal to (or, on par with) God's word but that the two things provide a God-given moral compass by which a person may navigate through life. God's word never changes; one's conscience, however, can change and can be recalibrated with a better understanding of God's word over time.

196 Barrett, *The Epistle to the Romans*, 266.

197 Adapted from Lenski, *Interpretation*, 818.

198 The Greek here is in a present active state: "that we might keep on having hope" (Robertson, *Word Pictures* [electronic], on 15:4).

199 "As the Jews glorify God for His faithfulness, so the Gentiles will glorify Him for His mercy" (Barrett, *The Epistle to the Romans*, 272).

200 Jesse was the father of David and provides the earthly lineage for both Joseph and Mary, Jesus' presumed father and His mother, respectively. The "root" (or "Branch") concept is repeated throughout the messianic prophecies of Christ, notably in Isaiah (4:2, 11:1, 27:6, 37:31, etc.); see also Jer. 23:5 and 33:15.

201 Perhaps the most critical remarks are found in Rom. 2:17–24, where Paul exposes the hypocrisy of the Jewish people, and possibly (by extension) some Jewish Christians. But these remarks are very general and do not target the Roman Christians themselves. Similar strong language is directed at Gentile Christians in 11:17–22, though these also are general remarks and do not appear to address a specific problem.

202 Lenski, *Interpretation*, 877.

203 "The word here translated minister is not *diakonos*, the usual word for minister, or servant, but *leitourgos*, a word that usually had an official significance, one who performs a public service" (Whiteside, *Commentary*, 285).

204 Barnes, *Notes* (electronic), on 15:21.

205 This negative sentiment is expressed in James' comments to Paul in Acts 21:17–21, which chronologically follows very shortly after Paul penned these very words in Romans. Yet Barnes' comments are instrumental here: "Nothing tends so much to wear off prejudice, and to prevent unkind feelings in regard to others, as to set about some purpose to do them good, or to unite with them in doing good" (*Notes* [electronic], on 15:26; emphases are his).

206 In Paul's perspective, "Rome was not a goal but a place which he must visit in transit, or at best a base from which he could set out on a further phase of his ministry, with a view to repeating in the western Mediterranean the program which (at the time indicated in Acts 19:21) he had almost completed in the East" (Bruce, "Romans," *Zondervan*, 150).

207 "The reception of the letter [i.e., to the Romans] may have had something to do with the welcome he received from some Roman Christians

as he approached their city along the Appian Way, when he was still some forty miles distant. 'The brethren there,' says his companion Luke, 'when they heard of us, came as far as the Forum of Appius and Three Taverns to meet us. On seeing them Paul thanked God and took courage' (Acts 28:15)" (Bruce, "Romans," *Zondervan*, 152; bracketed words are mine).

208 As to why Paul did not use a feminine Greek word to define Phoebe as a "deaconess" rather than simply a "deacon" is because the Greek language did not have such a word (J. N. D. Kelly, *The Pastoral Epistles* [Peabody, MA: Hendrickson Publishers, 1960], 83–84; bracketed words are mine).

209 Whiteside, *Commentary*, 296.

210 "This turning away amounted to a withdrawal of fellowship; and the withdrawal was to continue, so long as those withdrawn from continued to produce divisions. It was a separation of true brethren from false; and, without a reformation, it was final" (Lard, *Commentary*, 463).

211 Some information on Calvinism in this article is from: *Amazing Grace: The History and Theology of Calvinism* (DVD), Apologetics Group, © 2004; and David N. Steele and Curtis Thomas, http://the-highway.com/compare.html (2010).

212 In maintaining this process, Calvinism necessarily implies that one who is "born again" retains all his sins and guilt, since that person is then taught to take the necessary steps of repentance and seeking forgiveness. He is not "born again" pure and uncorrupted but is apparently re-born in his impurity and corruption.

213 "All sinned when Adam sinned. They sinned in him. … His act, for some good and proper reason, was regarded as their act … The act of the one legally binds the others. It is, in the eye of law and justice, their act" (Hodge, *Commentary*, 151). Thus, Adam sinned (he says) as a legal representative of humanity, making the entire human race guilty of what he did—even when (as in the case of children) no personal sin has been committed.

214 *The Canons of Dort,* 1618, as cited in *Amazing Grace* (DVD).

215 "Paul teaches clearly the doctrine of the personal election of men to eternal life, an election founded not on works, but on the good pleasure of God" (Hodge, *Commentary*, 323, in comments on Rom. 9). "This election is sovereign, i.e., is founded on the good pleasure of God, and not on any thing in its objects" (ibid.). Earlier, Hodge said that human faith is "required" for redemption (see fn. 75); here, he says God alone "elects" those whom He saves. Calvinists want to have it both ways, but this does not work.

216 For a fuller critique of Calvinism, I recommend chapter 17 ("Calvinism and Christianity") in my book, *The Gospel of Saving Grace* (Spiritbuilding Publishers, 2020); go to www.spiritbuilding.com/chad.

217 Summaries are from "Five Points of Calvinism" by Matthew J. Slick, © 1998–2006 (http://calvinistcorner.com/tulip.htm), cited April, 2010.

218 The parable of the prodigal son illustrates this (Luke 15:11–32). The prodigal son's own decision severed his fellowship with his father. Yet when the son "came to his senses," he returned to seek his father's forgiveness. The father's words are powerful: "This brother of yours was dead and has begun to live, and was lost and has been found." This father had always sought his son's fellowship; yet this fellowship could not have been restored until the son chose to pursue it.

219 Slick, *Calvinist Corner*.

220 *Ibid*.

221 *Amazing Grace* (DVD), on "Perseverance of the Saints."

www.ingramcontent.com/pod-product-compliance
Lightning Source LLC
Chambersburg PA
CBHW041925090426
42743CB00020B/3443